Collins

YO[RK]

CITY ATLAS

C000193729

Contents

Key to Street Map Symbols	2
Key to Street Map Pages	3
City Centre Map	4-5
Street Maps	6-27
Local Information	28-29
Places of Interest	30-33
The Minster	34
Key to Road Map Symbols	35
Road Map	36-37
Index to Street Names	38-48

Published by Collins
An imprint of HarperCollins*Publishers*
77-85 Fulham Palace Road, Hammersmith, London W6 8JB

The HarperCollins website address is: www.**fire**and**water**.com
Bartholomew website address is: www.bartholomewmaps.com
e-mail:roadcheck@harpercollins.co.uk

Mapping generated from Bartholomew digital databases

Copyright © HarperCollins*Publishers* Ltd 2001
Mapping © Bartholomew Ltd 2001

Collins® is a registered trademark of HarperCollins*Publishers* Limited

All rights reserved. No part of this publication may be reproduced, stored in a retrieval system, or transmitted, in any form or by any means, electronic, mechanical, photocopying, recording or otherwise, without the prior written permission of the publisher and copyright owners.

The contents of this publication are believed correct at the time of printing. Nevertheless, the publisher can accept no responsibility for errors or omissions, changes in the detail given, or for any expense or loss thereby caused.

The representation of a road, track or footpath is no evidence of a right of way.

Printed in Hong Kong ISBN 0 00 711052 9 NI10746 BDC

HarperCollins*Publishers*

Key to Street Map Symbols

A64	Primary road (dual/single)		Restricted access street
A19	'A' road (dual/single)		Pedestrian street
B1224	'B' road (dual/single)		Minor road/Track
	Other road (dual/single)	FB	Footpath/Cycle Path/ Footbridge
	Road under construction		Unitary authority boundary
Toll	One-way street/Toll		Postcode boundary
	Railway line		Bus/Coach station
	Level crossing/ Railway tunnel	P+	Park & Ride
	Railway station	P	Car Park
	Leisure/Tourism		Education
	Multiplex cinema		Health
	Shopping/Retail		Industry/Commerce
	Administration/Law		Notable building
Pol	Police station		Major religious building
PO	Post Office		Church/Mosque/ Synagogue
Lib	Library		Cinema
	Fire station/Ambulance station/Community centre		Theatre
WC	Public toilet	i i	Tourist information centre (all year/seasonal)
	Wood/Forest		Golf course
	Park/Garden/Recreation ground		Cemetery
	Public open space		Built up area
410	National Grid number	10	Page continuation number

SCALE: 4 inches to 1 mile (6.3 cm to 1 km)

0 – 1/4 – 1/2 – 3/4 – 1 mile

0 – 1/4 – 1/2 – 3/4 – 1 – 1 1/4 – 1 1/2 kilometres

SCALE (pages 4-5 only): 8 inches to 1 mile (12.6 cm to 1 km)

0 – 1/4 – 1/2 mile

0 – 1/4 – 1/2 – 3/4 kilometre

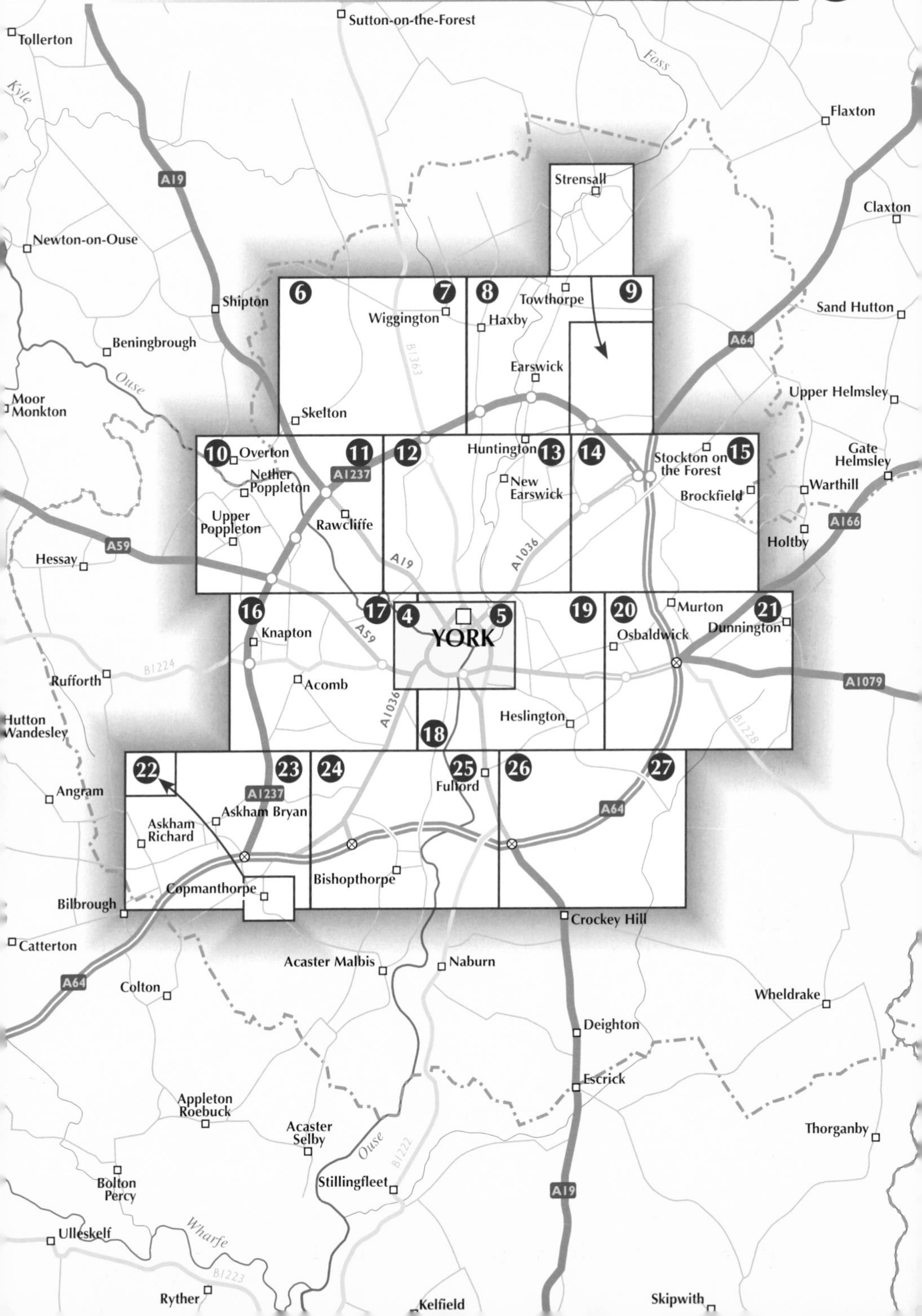
Foston
Sutton-on-the-Forest
Tollerton
Kyle
Foss
Flaxton
A19
Strensall
Claxton
Newton-on-Ouse
6
7
8
9
Wiggington
Towthorpe
Haxby
Sand Hutton
Shipton
Beningbrough
A64
B1363
Earswick
Ouse
Upper Helmsley
Moor Monkton
Skelton
10
Overton
11
12
Huntington
13
14
Stockton on the Forest
15
Gate Helmsley
Nether Poppleton
A1237
New Earswick
Warthill
Brockfield
Upper Poppleton
Rawcliffe
A166
Holtby
A59
A1036
Hessay
A19
16
17
4
YORK
5
19
20
Murton
21
Knapton
A59
Osbaldwick
Dunnington
B1224
Rufforth
Acomb
A1079
Hutton Wandesley
A1036
Heslington
B1228
18
22
23
24
25
26
27
Angram
A1237
Fulford
Askham Bryan
A64
Askham Richard
Bishopthorpe
Copmanthorpe
Bilbrough
Crockey Hill
Catterton
Acaster Malbis
Naburn
A64
Colton
Wheldrake
Deighton
Escrick
Appleton Roebuck
Acaster Selby
Thorganby
Ouse
B1222
Stillingfleet
Bolton Percy
A19
Ulleskelf
Wharfe
B1223
Ryther
Kelfield
Skipwith

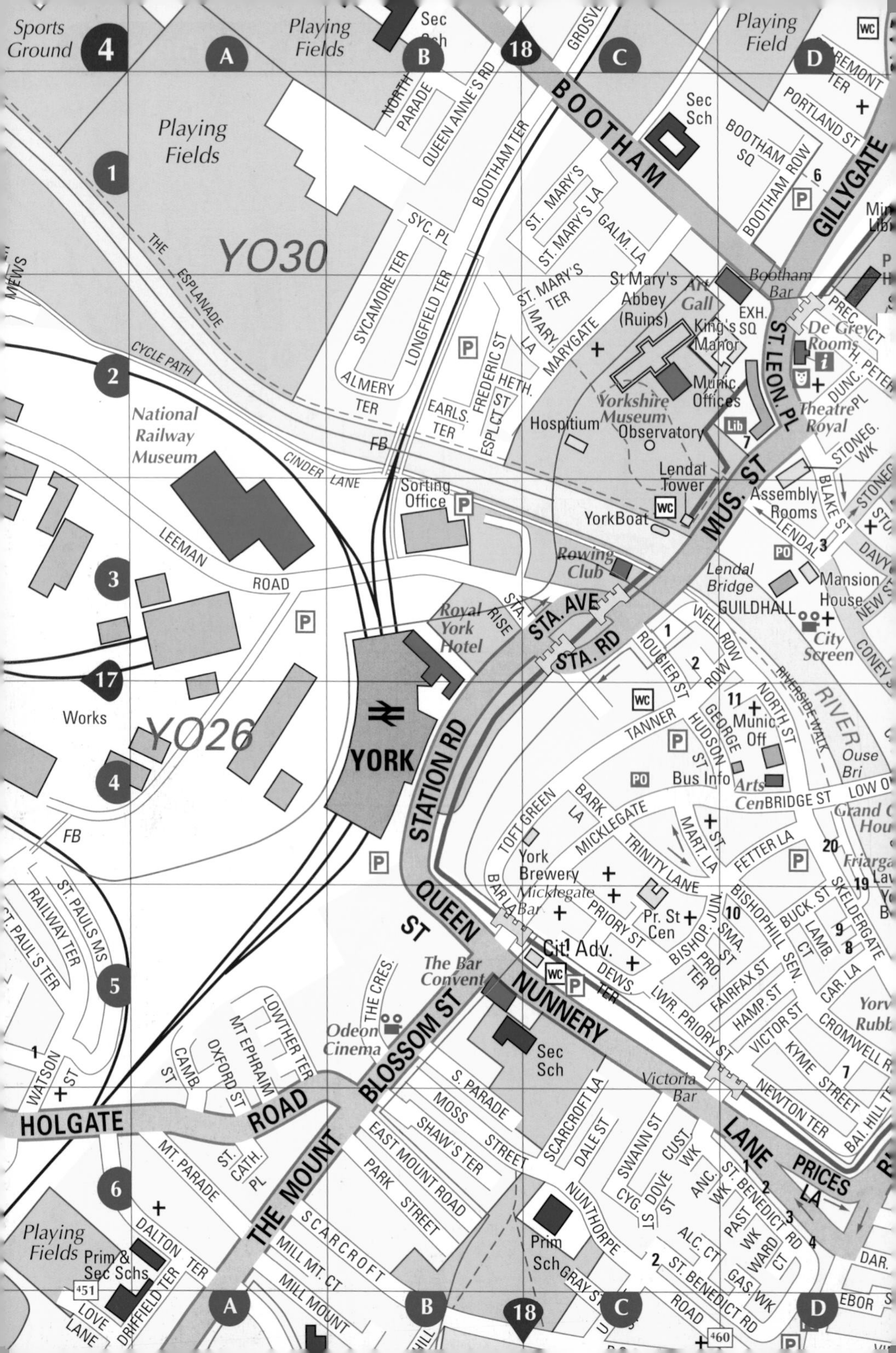

Sports Ground
Playing Fields
Playing Fields
Playing Field
Sec Sch
GROSVE
BOOTHAM
NORTH PARADE
QUEEN ANNE'S RD
BOOTHAM TER
CLAREMONT TER
PORTLAND ST
BOOTHAM SQ
BOOTHAM ROW
GILLYGATE
YO30
THE ESPLANADE
SYC. PL
SYCAMORE TER
LONGFIELD TER
ST. MARY'S
ST. MARY'S LA
GALM. LA
ST. MARY'S TER
MARY. LA
MARYGATE
St Mary's Abbey (Ruins)
Art Gall
Bootham Bar
EXH. SQ
King's Manor
ST. LEON. PL
PREC. CT
De Grey Rooms
H. PETER
CYCLE PATH
ALMERY TER
FREDERIC ST
HETH.
EARLS. TER
ESPL. CT
ST
Yorkshire Museum
Hospitium
Observatory
Munic. Offices
DUNC. PL
Theatre Royal
Lib
STONEG. WK
National Railway Museum
FB
CINDER LANE
Sorting Office
Lendal Tower
MUS. ST
Assembly Rooms
BLAKE ST
STONEG
YorkBoat
LENDAL
LEEMAN ROAD
Rowing Club
PO
Lendal Bridge
Mansion House
DAVY
ROAD
GUILDHALL
NEW ST
STA. RISE
STA. AVE
Royal York Hotel
STA. RD
WELL ROW
City Screen
CONEY
ROUGIER ST
ROW
RIVERSIDE WALK
RIVER Ouse
17
Works
YO26
TANNER
GEORGE HUDSON ST
Munic. Off
NORTH ST
Ouse Bri
YORK
STATION RD
PO
Bus Info
Arts Cen
BRIDGE ST
LOW O
TOFT GREEN
BARK. LA
MICKLEGATE
TRINITY LANE
MART. LA
ST.
FETTER LA
Grand Hou
FB
York Brewery
Micklegate Bar
BAR LA
PRIORY ST
Pr. St Cen
BISHOP. JUN.
SMA. ST
BISHOPHILL SEN.
BUCK. ST
SKELDERGATE
Friarga
QUEEN ST
ST. PAULS MS
RAILWAY TER
ST. PAUL'S TER
THE CRES.
The Bar Convent
Cit. Adv.
DEWS. TER
BISHOP. PRO. TER
FAIRFAX ST
LAMB. CT
CAR. LA
York Rubb
LOWTHER TER
MT EPHRAIM
OXFORD ST
CAMB. ST
Odeon Cinema
BLOSSOM ST
NUNNERY
LWR. PRIORY ST
HAMP. ST
VICTOR ST
CROMWELL R
KYME STREET
WATSON ST
Sec Sch
Victoria Bar
NEWTON TER
HOLGATE ROAD
S. PARADE
MOSS STREET
SCARCROFT LA
DALE ST
SWANN ST
CUST. WK
LANE
PRICES LA
BAI. HILL TER
ST. CATH. PL
MT. PARADE
EAST MOUNT ROAD
SHAW'S TER
DOVE ST
ANC. WK
ST. BENEDICT RD
THE MOUNT
PARK STREET
NUNTHORPE
CYG. ST
PAST. WK
WARD CT
SCARCROFT
Prim Sch
ALC. CT
DALTON TER
Playing Fields
Prim & Sec Schs
MILL MT. CT
GRAY ST
ST. BENEDICT RD
GAS. WK
DAR.
MILL MOUNT
ROAD
EBOR
451
LOVE LANE
DRIFFIELD TER
460
A
B
C
D
18
1
2
3
4
5
6

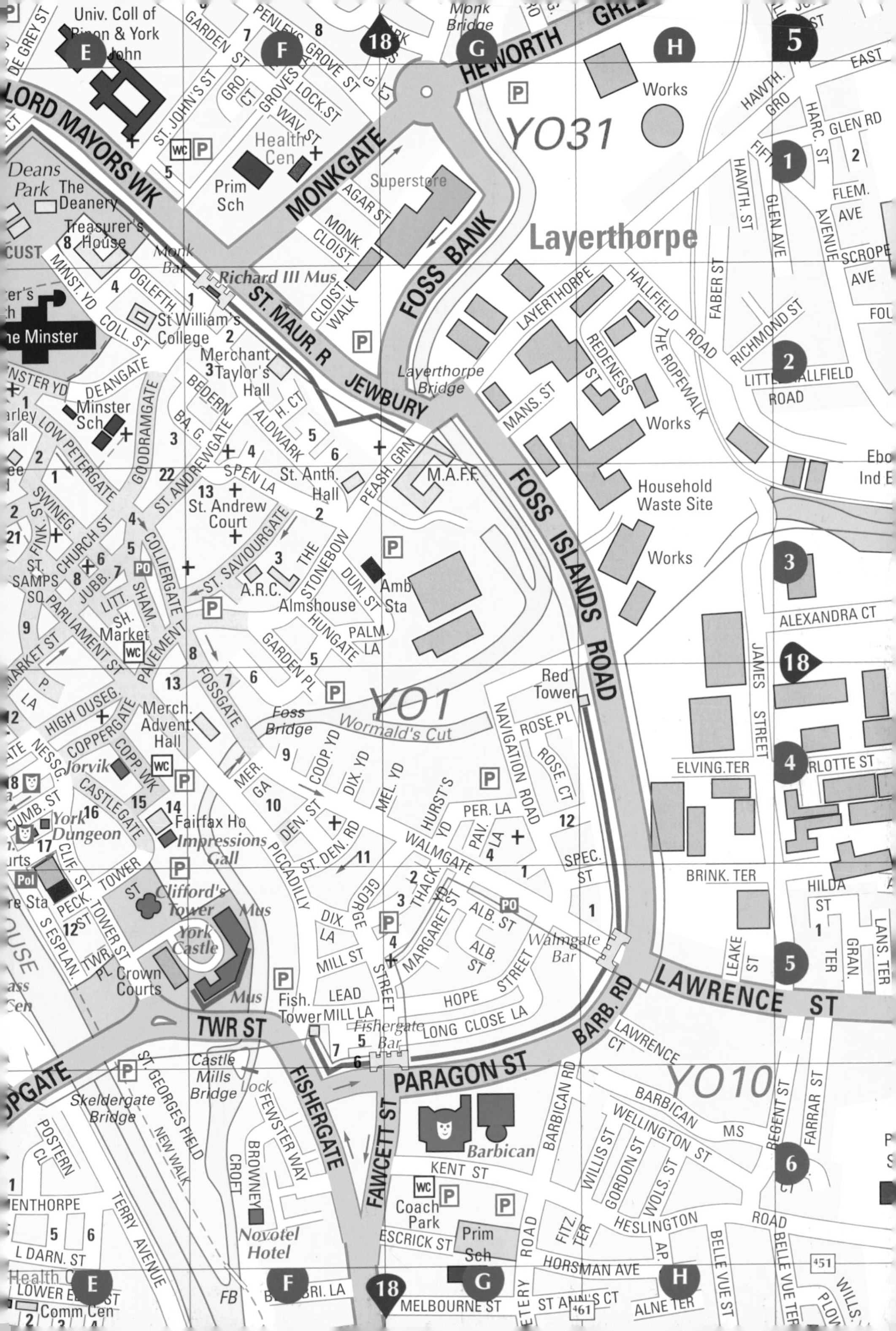

E
F
G
H
5
18
Univ. Coll of Ripon & York St. John
DE GREY ST
GARDEN ST
PENLEYS GROVE ST
Monk Bridge
HEWORTH GREEN
LORD MAYORS WK
ST. JOHN'S ST
GRO. CT.
GROVES LA
LOCK ST
WAV. ST
Health Cen
Prim Sch
MONKGATE
Superstore
AGAR ST
MONK. CLOIST.
FOSS BANK
Works
YO31
HAWTH. GRO
HARC. ST
GLEN RD
EAST
FIFTH
HAWTH. ST
GLEN AVE
AVENUE
FLEM. AVE
SCROPE AVE
Layerthorpe
Deans Park
The Deanery
Treasurer's House
CUST
Monk Bar
Richard III Mus
MINST. YD
OGLEFTH.
St William's College
Merchant Taylor's Hall
The Minster
COLL. ST
DEANGATE
ST. MAUR. R
CLOIST. WALK
JEWBURY
Layerthorpe Bridge
LAYERTHORPE
HALLFIELD ROAD
REDENESS ST
THE ROPEWALK
FABER ST
RICHMOND ST
LITTLE HALLFIELD ROAD
MANS. ST
Works
Minster Sch
Barley Hall
LOW PETERGATE
GOODRAMGATE
BEDERN
BA. G.
H. CT
ALDWARK
ST. ANDREWGATE
SPEN LA
St. Anth. Hall
PEASH. GRN
M.A.F.F.
FOSS ISLANDS ROAD
Household Waste Site
Ebor Ind E
St. Andrew Court
SWINEG.
FINK. ST
CHURCH ST
COLLIERGATE
ST. SAVIOURGATE
THE STONEBOW
DUN. ST
Amb Sta
Works
3
ST. SAMPS SQ.
JUBB.
LITT. SH.
SHAM.
PO
A.R.C.
Almshouse
HUNGATE
PALM. LA
ALEXANDRA CT
PARLIAMENT ST
Market
WC
PAVEMENT
FOSSGATE
GARDEN PL
MARKET ST
JAMES STREET
Red Tower
P. LA
HIGH OUSEG.
Merch. Advent. Hall
Foss Bridge
YO1
Wormald's Cut
NAVIGATION ROAD
ROSE. PL
ROSE. CT
NESSG.
COPPERGATE
COPP. WK
Jorvik
MER. GA
COOP. YD
DIX. YD
MEL. YD
HURST'S YD
ELVING. TER
CHARLOTTE ST
4
CASTLEGATE
CUMB. ST
York Dungeon
Fairfax Ho
Impressions Gall
DEN. ST
ST. DEN. RD
PICCADILLY
WALMGATE
PER. LA
PAV. LA
SPEC. ST
CLIF. ST
Pol
PECK. ST
TOWER ST
S ESPLAN.
TWR. PL
Clifford's Tower
Mus
York Castle
Crown Courts
GEORGE ST
DIX. LA
MILL ST
THACK. YD
MARGARET ST
ALB. ST
Walmgate Bar
HOPE STREET
LEAKE ST
BRINK. TER
HILDA ST
TER
GRAN.
LANS. TER
LAWRENCE ST
BARB. RD
Fish. Tower
LEAD MILL LA
Fishergate Bar
LONG CLOSE LA
LAWRENCE CT
TWR ST
OPGATE
Skeldergate Bridge
ST. GEORGES FIELD
Castle Mills Bridge
Lock
FISHERGATE
FAWCETT ST
PARAGON ST
Barbican
BARBICAN RD
BARBICAN MS
YO10
WELLINGTON ST
REGENT ST
FARRAR ST
6
POSTERN CL
NEW WALK
FEWSTER WAY
BROWNEY CROFT
KENT ST
WILLIS ST
GORDON ST
WOLS. ST
TERRY AVENUE
Coach Park
Prim Sch
ESCRICK ST
ROAD
FITZ. TER
HESLINGTON ROAD
AP.
BELLE VUE ST
BELLE VUE TER
Novotel Hotel
ENTHORPE
L DARN. ST
Health Cen
LOWER EL. ST
Comm Cen
FB
BRI. LA
HORSMAN AVE
MELBOURNE ST
ST ANN'S CT
ALNE TER
CEMETERY
451
461
WILLS.
PLOW.

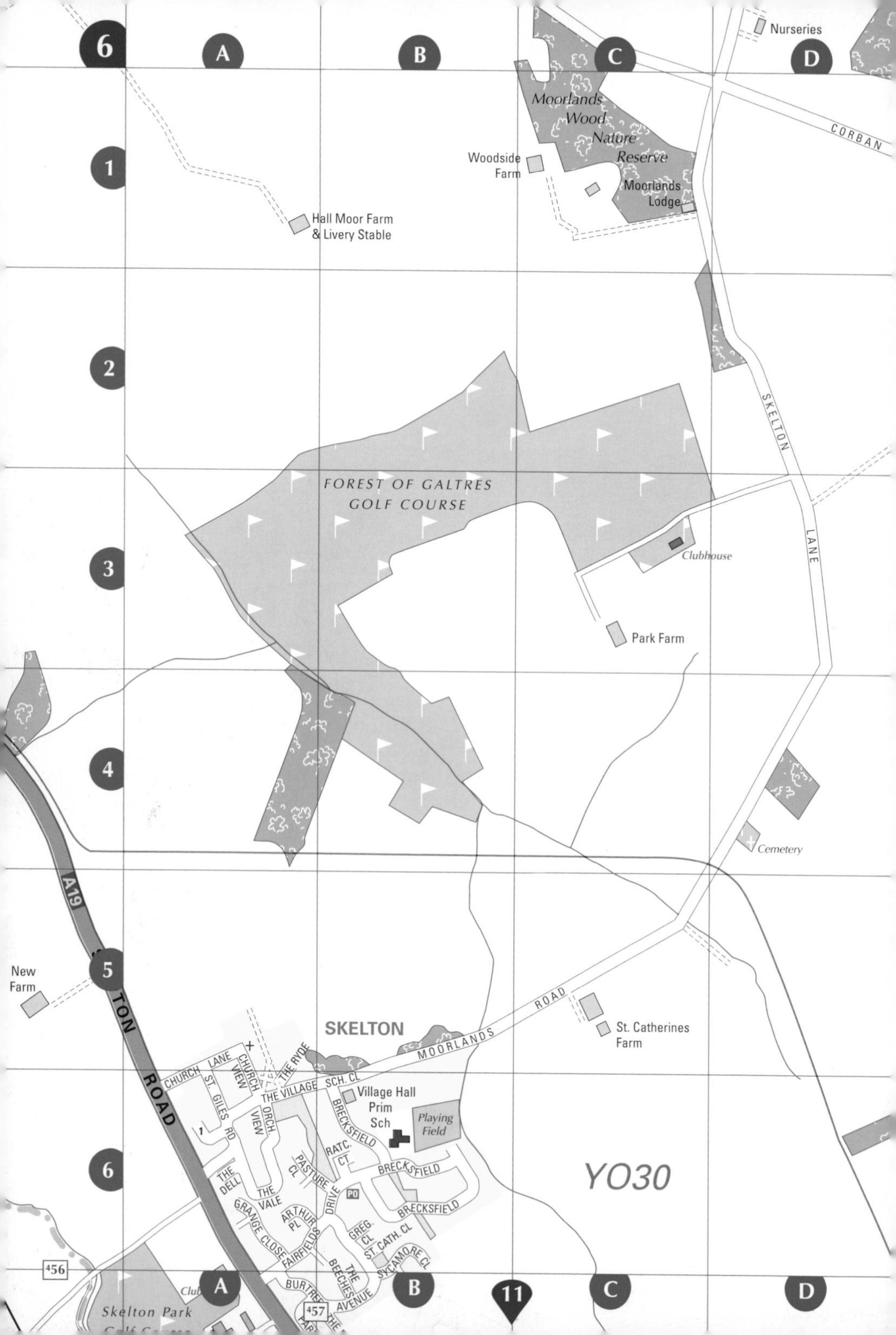
6
A
B
C
D
1
2
3
4
5
6
Nurseries
Moorlands Wood Nature Reserve
CORBAN
Woodside Farm
Moorlands Lodge
Hall Moor Farm & Livery Stable
SKELTON LANE
FOREST OF GALTRES GOLF COURSE
Clubhouse
Park Farm
Cemetery
A19
New Farm
SKELTON ROAD
MOORLANDS ROAD
SKELTON
St. Catherines Farm
CHURCH LANE
CHURCH VIEW
THE RYDE
ST. GILES RD
THE VILLAGE
SCH. CL
Village Hall
Prim Sch
Playing Field
BRECKSFIELD
ORCH. VIEW
RATC. CT
PASTURE CL
THE DELL
THE VALE
DRIVE
PO
GRANGE CLOSE
ARTHUR PL
FAIRFIELDS
GREG. CL
ST. CATH. CL
SYCAMORE CL
THE BEECHES
AVENUE
BURTREE
YO30
456
457
11
Skelton Park Golf Course

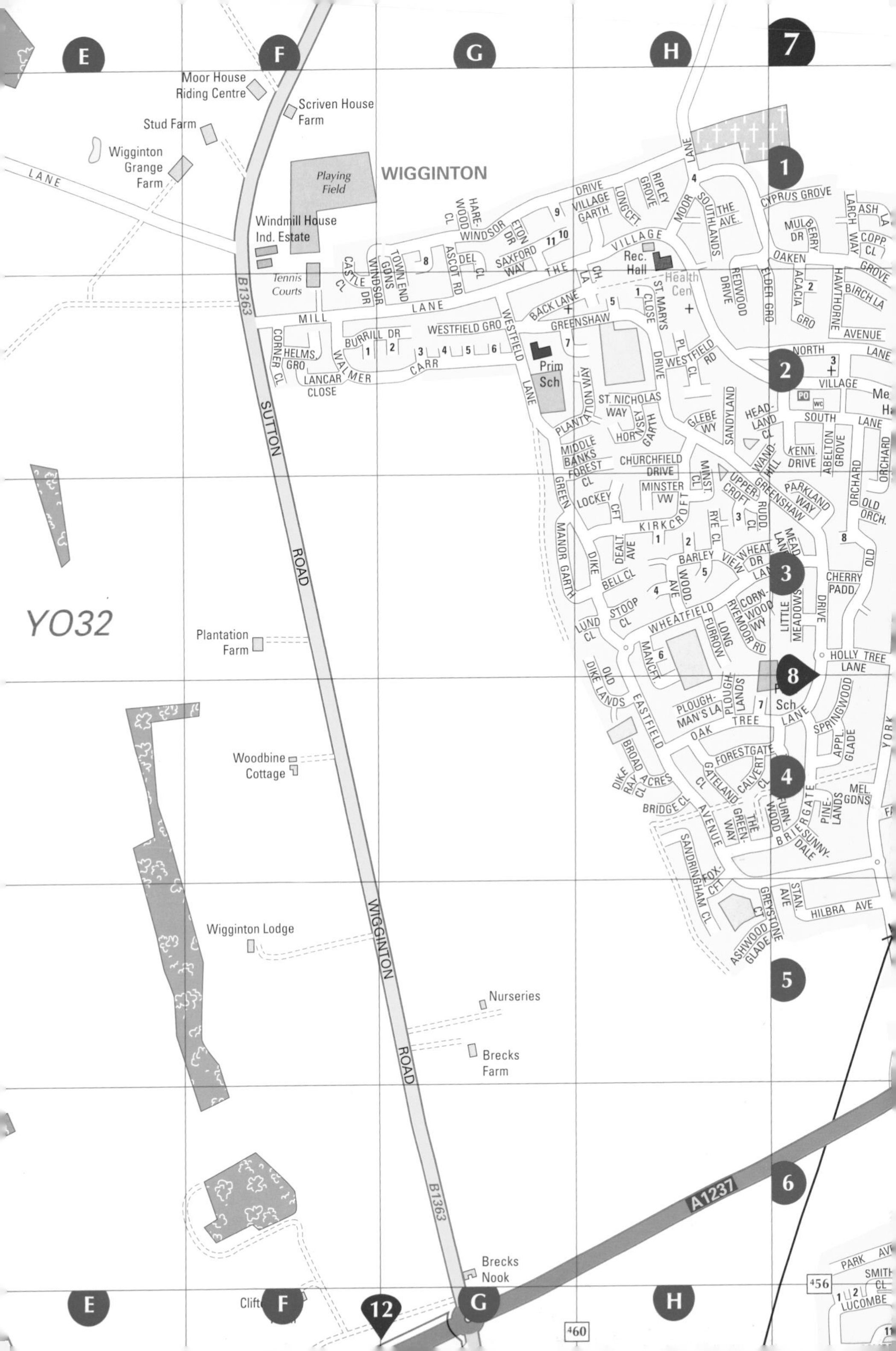

E
F
G
H
7
Moor House Riding Centre
Scriven House Farm
Stud Farm
Wigginton Grange Farm
LANE
WIGGINTON
Playing Field
Windmill House Ind. Estate
Tennis Courts
B1363
MILL LANE
CORNER CL
HELMS GRO
LANCAR CLOSE
WALMER CARR
BURRILL DR
WESTFIELD GRO
WESTFIELD LANE
CASTLE DR
WINDSOR GDNS
TOWN END
ASCOT RD
DEL CL
HAREWOOD CL
WINDSOR DR
ETON DR
SAXFORD WAY
THE VILLAGE
DRIVE
VILLAGE GARTH
LONGCFT.
RIPLEY GROVE
MOOR LANE
SOUTHLANDS
THE AVE.
CH. LA
BACK LANE
GREENSHAW
Rec. Hall
Health Cen
ST. MARYS CLOSE
DRIVE
WESTFIELD PL
WESTFIELD CL
RD
Prim Sch
PLANTATION WAY
ST. NICHOLAS WAY
HORSEY GARTH
MIDDLE BANKS
FOREST CL
GREEN
CHURCHFIELD DRIVE
MINSTER VW
MINST. CL
LOCKEY CFT
KIRKCROFT
MANOR GARTH
DIKE
DEALT. AVE
BELL CL
STOOP CL
WOOD AVE
BARLEY VIEW
RYE CL
UPPER CROFT
RUDD. CL
WHEAT. DR
WHEATFIELD LANE
LONG FURROW
RYEMOOR RD
CORNWOOD WY
LUND CL
OLD DIKE LANDS
MANCFT.
EASTFIELD
PLOUGHMAN'S LA
PLOUGHLANDS
OAK TREE LANE
Sch
BROAD ACRES
DIKE RAY CL
BRIDGE CL
FORESTGATE
GATELAND CL
CALVERT CL
AVENUE
GREENWAY
THE GREEN.
FURNWOOD
SANDRINGHAM CL.
FOXCFT
GREYSTONE CT
ASHWOOD GLADE
STAN. AVE
HILBRA AVE
CYPRUS GROVE
MULBERRY DR
LARCH WAY
ASH LA
COPP. CL
OAKEN GROVE
ACACIA GRO
HAWTHORNE AVENUE
BIRCH LA
REDWOOD DRIVE
ELDER GRO
NORTH LANE
VILLAGE
SOUTH LANE
PO
WC
SANDYLAND
HEADLAND CL
GLEBE WY
WANDHILL
KENN. DRIVE
ABELTON GROVE
ORCHARD
PARKLAND WAY
GREENSHAW
MEAD LANE
OLD ORCH.
CHERRY PADD.
LITTLE MEADOWS
DRIVE
HOLLY TREE LANE
SPRINGWOOD
APPL. GLADE
MEL. GDNS
PINELANDS
BRIERGATE
SUNNYDALE
YORK
YO32
SUTTON ROAD
Plantation Farm
Woodbine Cottage
Wigginton Lodge
WIGGINTON ROAD
Nurseries
Brecks Farm
Brecks Nook
A1237
PARK AVE
SMITH CL
LUCOMBE
456
460
12
1
2
3
4
5
6
8

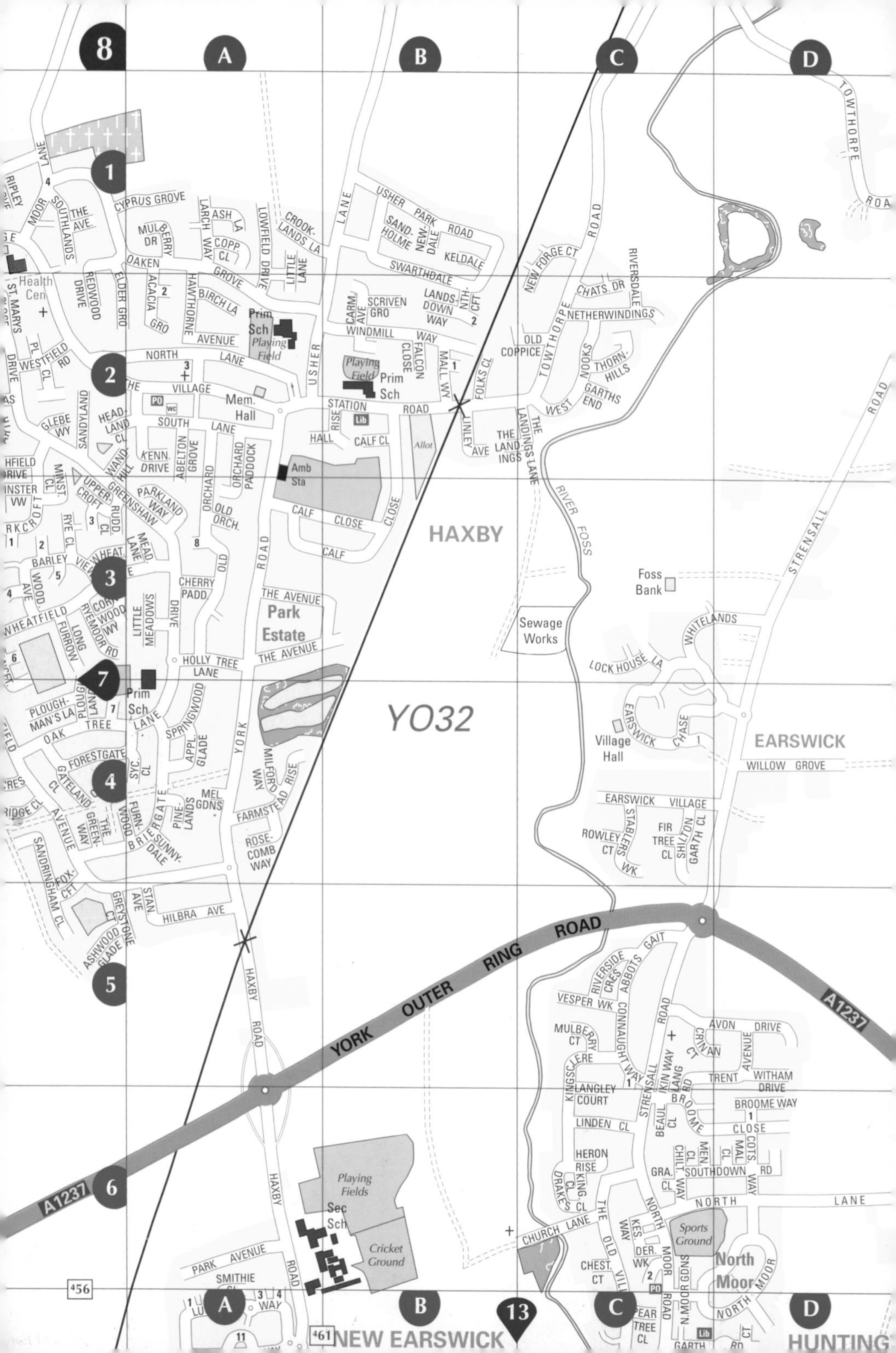
8
A
B
C
D
1
2
3
4
5
6
7
13
HAXBY
YO32
EARSWICK
NEW EARSWICK
HUNTING
456
461
YORK OUTER RING ROAD
A1237
HAXBY ROAD
YORK ROAD
STRENSALL ROAD
TOWTHORPE ROAD
RIVER FOSS
Park Estate
THE AVENUE
USHER LANE
USHER PARK ROAD
NORTH LANE
THE VILLAGE
SOUTH LANE
STATION ROAD
CALF CLOSE
CALF CL
CYPRUS GROVE
OAKEN GROVE
HAWTHORNE AVENUE
LOWFIELD DRIVE
CROOKLANDS LA
LITTLE LANE
BIRCH LA
WINDMILL WAY
SWARTHDALE
KELDALE
SANDHOLME
NEWDALE
LANDSDOWN WAY
SCRIVEN GRO
CARM. AVE
FALCON CLOSE
MALL. WY
FOLKS CL
LINLEY AVE
THE LANDINGS
THE LANDINGS LANE
NEW FORGE CT
CHATS. DR
RIVERSDALE
NETHERWINDINGS
OLD COPPICE
NOOKS
THORNHILLS
GARTHS END
WEST
Health Cen
Prim Sch
Playing Field
Mem. Hall
PO
wc
Lib
Amb Sta
Allot
Foss Bank
Sewage Works
Village Hall
WHITELANDS
LOCK HOUSE LA
EARSWICK CHASE
WILLOW GROVE
EARSWICK VILLAGE
ROWLEY CT
STABLERS WK
FIR TREE CL
SHILTON GARTH CL
RIPLEY
MOOR LANE
SOUTHLANDS
THE AVE.
REDWOOD DRIVE
ELDER GRO
ACACIA GRO
MULBERRY DR
ASH LA
LARCH WAY
COPP. CL
ST. MARYS
WESTFIELD PL
WESTFIELD RD
GLEBE WY
SANDYLAND
HEADLAND CL
WANDHILL
KENN. DRIVE
ABELTON GROVE
ORCHARD PADDOCK
ORCHARD
OLD ORCH.
MINST. CL
UPPERCROFT
GREENSHAW
PARKLAND WAY
RUDD. CL
RYE CL
BARLEY VIEW
WHEAT. MEAD. LANE
CHERRY PADD.
WOOD. AVE
WHEATFIELD
LONG FURROW
RYEMOOR RD
CORNWOOD WY
LITTLE MEADOWS
DRIVE
HOLLY TREE LANE
PLOUGHMAN'S LA
OAK TREE LANE
SPRINGWOOD
APPL. GLADE
MILFORD WAY
FARMSTEAD RISE
ROSECOMB WAY
FORESTGATE
GATELAND CL
SYC. CL
AVENUE
THE GREENWAY
FURNWOOD
BRIERGATE
PINELANDS
SUNNYDALE
MEL. GDNS
SANDRINGHAM CL
FOX. CFT
GREYSTONE CT
ASHWOOD GLADE
STAN. AVE
HILBRA AVE
Playing Fields
Sec Sch
Cricket Ground
PARK AVENUE
SMITHIE CL
WAY
RIVERSIDE CRES
ABBOTS GAIT
VESPER WK
CONNAUGHT WAY
MULBERRY CT
KINGSCLERE
LANGLEY COURT
LINDEN CL
HERON RISE
KING. CL
DRAKE'S CL
CHURCH LANE
THE OLD VILLAGE
AVON DRIVE
CRINAN CT
AVENUE
TRENT
WITHAM DRIVE
BROOME WAY
BROOME CLOSE
BEAUL CL
CHILT. WAY
MEN. CL
MAL. CL
COTS. WAY
SOUTHDOWN RD
GRA. CL
NORTH LANE
Sports Ground
North Moor
NORTH MOOR
KES. WAY
DER. WK
MOOR ROAD
N. MOOR GDNS
CHEST. CT
PEAR TREE CL
GARTH RD

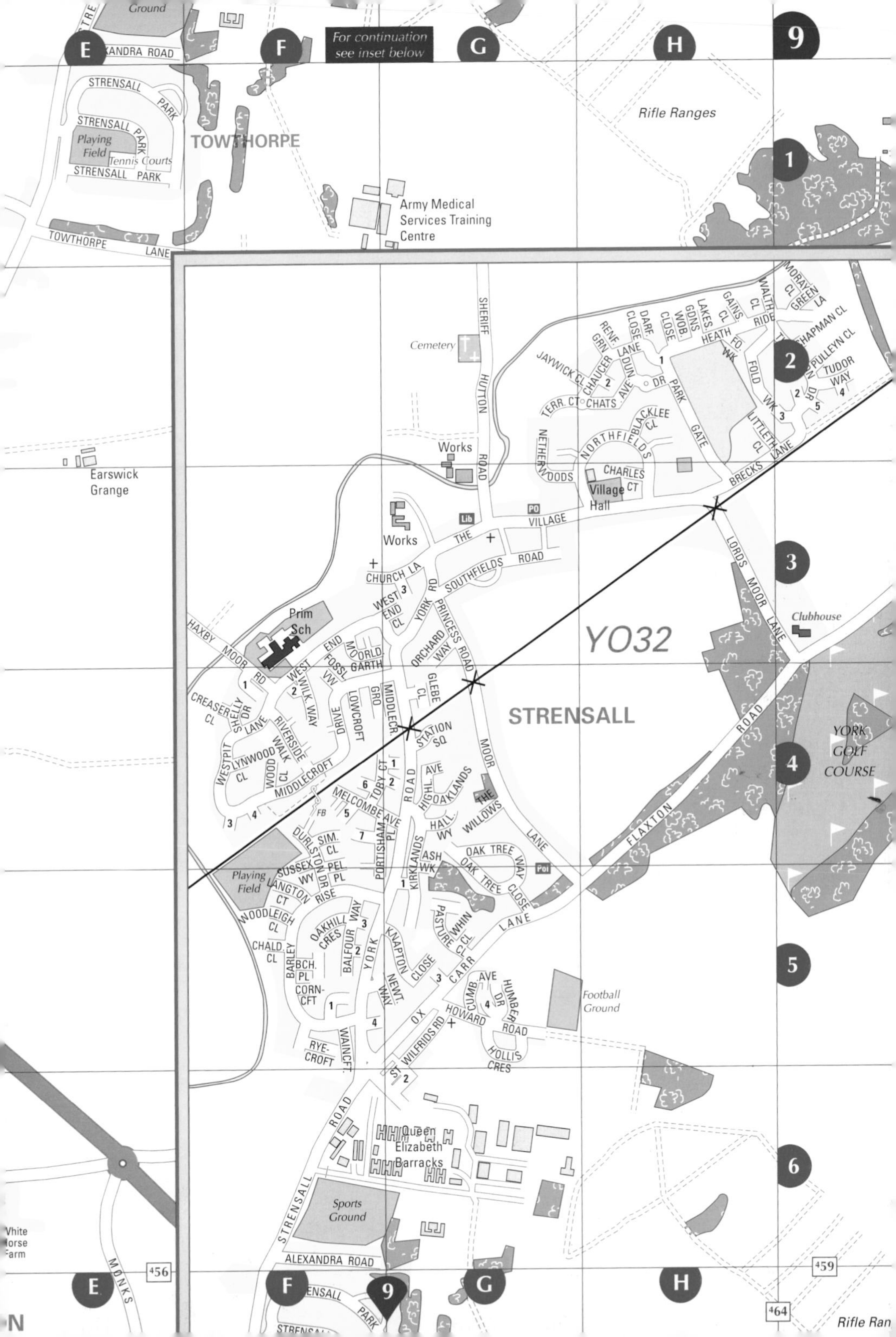

9
E
F
G
H
For continuation see inset below
ALEXANDRA ROAD
STRENSALL PARK
Playing Field
Tennis Courts
TOWTHORPE
TOWTHORPE LANE
Army Medical Services Training Centre
Rifle Ranges
1
2
3
4
5
6
SHERIFF HUTTON ROAD
Cemetery
Works
Earswick Grange
JAYWICK CL
CHAUCER LANE
DUN. AVE
DR
PARK GATE
LAKES. GDNS
WOB. CLOSE
DARF. CLOSE
RENF. GRN
GAINS. CL
HEATH RIDE
FO. WK
FOLD WK
WALTH. CL
MORAY CL
GREEN LA
CHAPMAN CL
PULLEYN CL
TUDOR WAY
DR
LITTLETH. CL
BRECKS LANE
TERR. CT
CHATS
BLACKLEE CL
NORTHFIELDS
NETHERWOODS
CHARLES CT
Village Hall
PO
Lib
THE VILLAGE
SOUTHFIELDS ROAD
CHURCH LA
WEST END CL
YORK RD
PRINCESS ROAD
ORCHARD WAY
GLEBE CL
LORDS MOOR LANE
Clubhouse
YO32
STRENSALL
YORK GOLF COURSE
Prim Sch
HAXBY MOOR RD
WEST END
MOORLD. GARTH
FOSSL. VW
WEST. WILK. WAY
CREASER CL
SHELLY DR
LANE
RIVERSIDE WALK
LOWCROFT DRIVE
GRO
MIDDLECR.
STATION SQ
WESTPIT LANE
LYNWOOD CL
WOOD CL
MIDDLECROFT
FB
MELCOMBE AVE
TOBY CT
ROAD
HIGHL. AVE
OAKLANDS
THE WILLOWS
MOOR LANE
FLAXTON ROAD
HALL WY
OAK TREE WAY
OAK TREE CLOSE
Pol
DURLSTON DR
SIM. CL
PEL PL
PORTISHAM PL
KIRKLANDS
ASH WK
Playing Field
SUSSEX WY
LANGTON CT
RISE
WOODLEIGH CL
OAKHILL CRES
BALFOUR WAY
YORK
KNAPTON CLOSE
PASTURE CL
WHIN CL
LANE
CARR
OX
CHALD. CL
BARLEY
BCH. PL
CORN-CFT
NEWT. WAY
CUMB. AVE
HUMBER DR
HOWARD ROAD
Football Ground
ST. WILFRIDS RD
HOLLIS CRES
RYE-CROFT
WAINCFT.
ROAD
Queen Elizabeth Barracks
STRENSALL
Sports Ground
ALEXANDRA ROAD
White Horse Farm
MONKS
456
459
464
STRENSALL PARK
N
Rifle Ran

A
B
C
D
1
2
3
4
5
6
OVERTON
New Farm Estate
RIVER OUSE
UPPER POPPLETON
YO26
Sports Ground
Comm Cen
Bowls Club
Lib
Prim Sch
Playing Field
MAIN STREET
PO
FOX GARTH
POPPLETON HALL GDNS
CHURCH LANE
RIVERSIDE WALK
RIVERSIDE GDNS
LITTLEFIELD CL
RIVERSVALE DR
BANKSIDE CL
SPRINGFIELD RD
WAY
HAWTH. CL
HILLCREST AVENUE
MILLFIELD
Allot
HUT. CL
MILLFIELD GDNS
NURSERY CT
NETHER WAY
MONTAGUE WALK
ALLERTON DRIVE
LITTLE GARTH
NURSERY RD
EBOR CL
DIKELANDS LANE
EBOR
PEAR TREE AVE
SCHOOL LA
STREET
BEECH WAY
ELM TREE AVE
MIDWAY AVE
EASTHORPE DR
LIME GARTH
APPLE GAR.
SANDYRIDGE LANE
CHANTRY GAP
CHANT. AVE
CHANT. GRO
ORCHARD ROAD
LONGRIDGE DR
LINT. RD
LONG RIDGE LANE
BRACKENHILLS
FAIRWAY DR
SYCAMORE VIEW
DIKELANDS CLOSE
LANE
WESTFIELD LANE
NETHER POPPLETON
THE GREEN
BEECH GRO
WESTF. CL
COPPER BEECH CL
THE MANOR CT
MANOR CLOSE
STATION ROAD
WILL. CFT
HODGSON LANE
BLACK DIKE LANE
Grange Farm
Crescent Farm
Red Lion Inn
POPPLETON
A59
BOROUGHBRIDGE ROAD
A1237
BURLANDS ROAD
Garden Centre
FIELD LANE
Prospect Farm
453
455
16

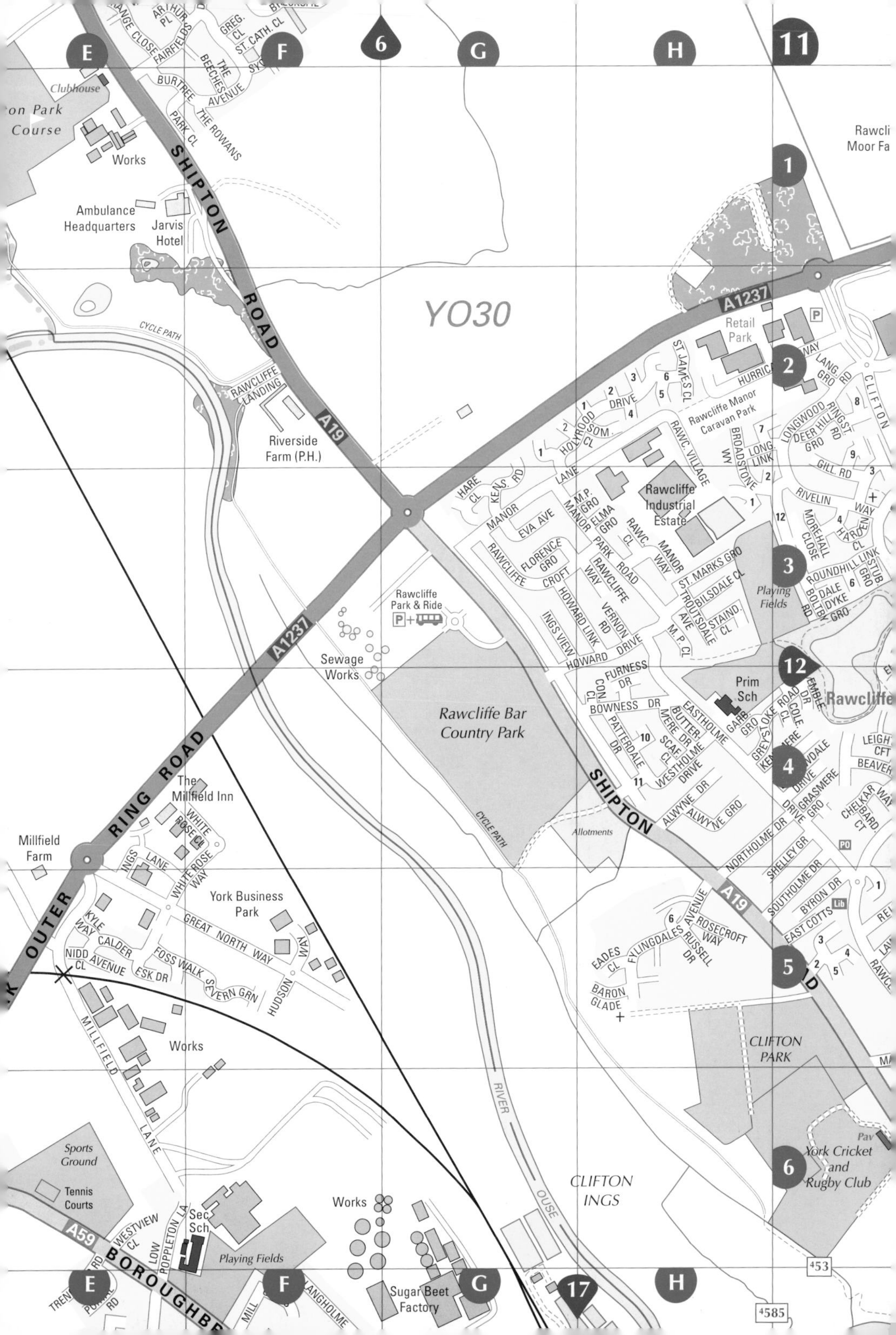
E
F
6
G
H
Clubhouse
Works
Ambulance Headquarters
Jarvis Hotel
SHIPTON ROAD
A19
A1237
YO30
CYCLE PATH
RAWCLIFFE LANDING
Riverside Farm (P.H.)
Rawcliffe Moor Fa
Retail Park
Rawcliffe Manor Caravan Park
Rawcliffe Industrial Estate
Rawcliffe Park & Ride
Sewage Works
Rawcliffe Bar Country Park
Playing Fields
Prim Sch
Allotments
OUTER RING ROAD
The Millfield Inn
Millfield Farm
York Business Park
GREAT NORTH WAY
Works
MILLFIELD LANE
CLIFTON PARK
York Cricket and Rugby Club
Pav
RIVER OUSE
CLIFTON INGS
Sports Ground
Tennis Courts
A59
BOROUGHBRIDGE
Sec Sch
Playing Fields
Works
Sugar Beet Factory
17
1
2
3
4
5
6
12
453
4585

12
A
B
7
C
D
Cliftongate Farm
Rawcliffe Moor Farm
YORK OUTER RING ROAD
A1237
Retail Park
Clifton Moor Retail Park
STIRLING ROAD
Warner Village Cinema
North York Trading Estate
Pioneer Business Park
Driving Range
WIGGINTON ROAD
Rawcliffe Manor Caravan Park
Rawcliffe Industrial Estate
Clifton Moor Bus. Village
Marsden Park
Centurion Park
CLIFTON MOOR GATE
Prim Sch
Playing Fields
Caravan Park
Rawcliffe
Green Lane Trading Estate
YO30
BOOTHAM STRAY
Allotments
B1363
KINGSWAY NORTH
A19
CLIFTON PARK
York Cricket and Rugby Club
Pav
Sec Sch
Tennis Courts
Comm Cen
Health Cen
Lib
PO
CLIFTON
Clifton
Youth Hostel
GROSVENOR ROAD
YORK DISTRICT HOSPITAL
17
453
4585

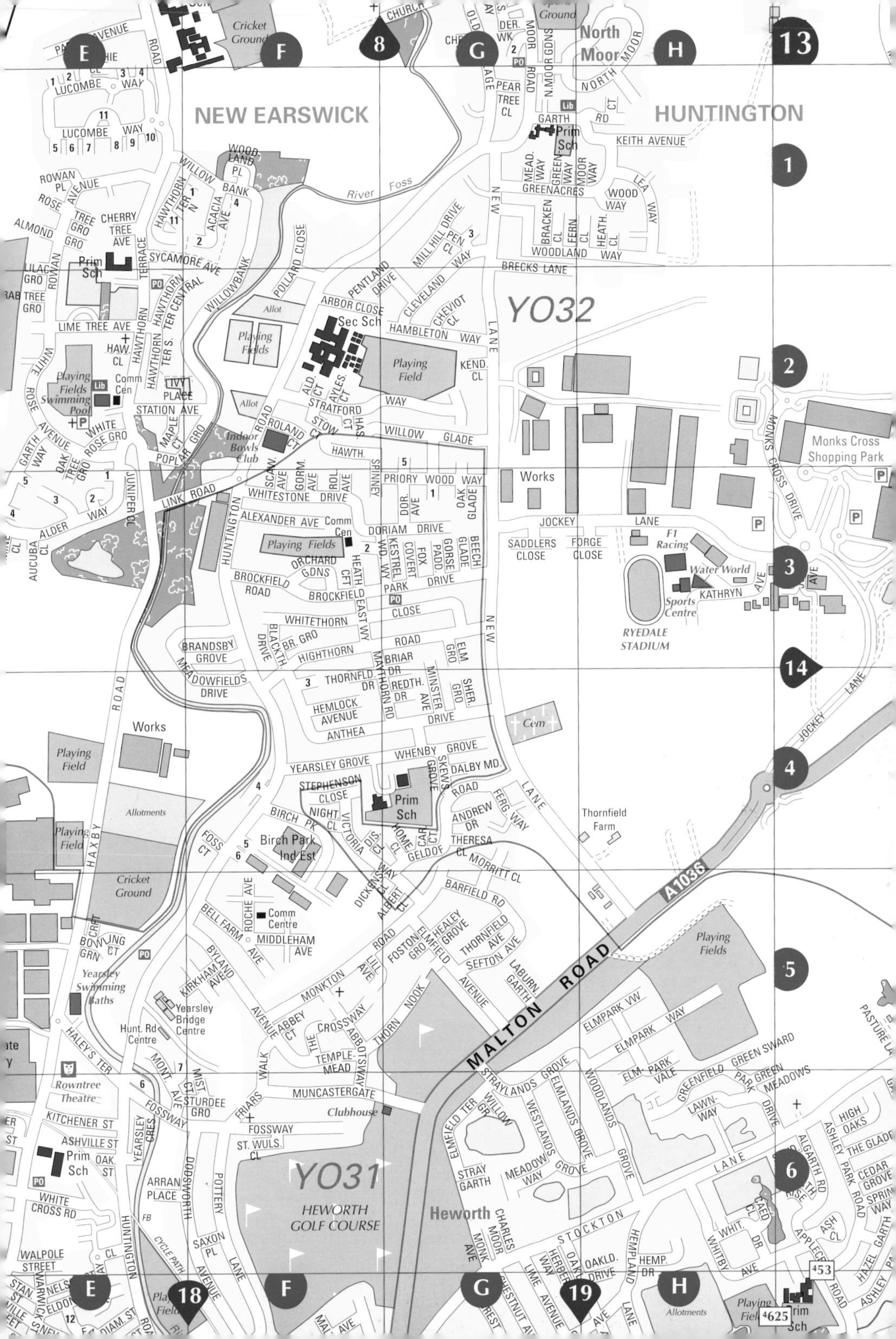

13
E
F
G
H
8
NEW EARSWICK
HUNTINGTON
North Moor
Cricket Ground
LUCOMBE WAY
ROWAN PL
ROWAN AVENUE
ROSE TREE GRO
CHERRY TREE AVE
ALMOND GRO
LILAC GRO
CRAB TREE GRO
Prim Sch
SYCAMORE AVE
TERRACE
WILLOW BANK
WOODLAND PL
HAWTHORN TER N
ACACIA AVE
River Foss
WILLOWBANK
POLLARD CLOSE
LIME TREE AVE
HAW. CL
Playing Fields
Swimming Pool
Lib
Comm Cen
STATION AVE
IVY PLACE
MAPLE CT
POPLAR GRO
WHITE ROSE AVENUE
WHITE ROSE GRO
GARTH WAY
OAK TREE GRO
JUNIPER CL
ALDER WAY
AUCUBA CL
LINK ROAD
Indoor Bowls Club
ROLAND CT
HUNTINGTON ROAD
Allot
Playing Fields
Sec Sch
ARBOR CLOSE
PENTLAND DRIVE
CLEVELAND WAY
CHEVIOT CL
HAMBLETON WAY
KEND. CL
Playing Field
STRATFORD WAY
STOW CT
WILLOW GLADE
HAWTH. SPINNEY
PRIORY WOOD WAY
OAK GLADE
WHITESTONE DRIVE
ALEXANDER AVE
DORIAM DRIVE
Playing Fields
ORCHARD GDNS
BROCKFIELD ROAD
BROCKFIELD PARK DRIVE
KESTREL WD. WY
FOX COVERT
GORSE PADD.
BEECH GLADE
WHITETHORN CLOSE
ROAD
BLACKTH. DRIVE
BR. GRO
HIGHTHORN
BRIAR DR
ELM GRO
BRANDSBY GROVE
MEADOWFIELDS DRIVE
THORNFLD. DR
REDTH. DR
MAYTHORN RD
MINSTER AVE
SHER. GRO
HEMLOCK AVENUE
ANTHEA DRIVE
YEARSLEY GROVE
WHENBY GROVE
DALBY MD.
STEPHENSON CLOSE
NIGHT. CL
VICTORIA WAY
Prim Sch
BIRCH PK
HOME CL
ANDREW DR
FERG. WAY
THERESA CL
GELDOF
MORRITT CL
Birch Park Ind Est
FOSS CT
DICKENS CL
ALBERT CL
BARFIELD RD
Comm Centre
ROCHE AVE
BELL FARM AVE
MIDDLEHAM AVE
BYLAND AVE
KIRKHAM AVE
MONKTON ROAD
LILL AVE
FOSTON GRO
ELMFIELD AVENUE
HEALEY GROVE
THORNFIELD AVE
SEFTON AVE
LABURN GARTH
MALTON ROAD
A1036
Playing Fields
ABBEY CT
THE CROSSWAY
ABBOTSWAY
TEMPLEMEAD
THORN NOOK
MUNCASTERGATE
Clubhouse
FRIARS WALK
FOSSWAY
ST. WULS. CL
YO31
HEWORTH GOLF COURSE
Heworth
Works
Playing Field
Allotments
Playing Field
HAXBY ROAD
Cricket Ground
BOWLING GRN
CRFT
Yearsley Swimming Baths
Yearsley Bridge Centre
Hunt. Rd Centre
HALEY'S TER
Rowntree Theatre
KITCHENER ST
ASHVILLE ST
Prim Sch
OAK. ST
YEARSLEY CRES
WHITE CROSS RD
WALPOLE STREET
ARRAN PLACE
POTTERY LANE
DODSWORTH AVENUE
SAXON PL
HUNTINGTON ROAD
CYCLE PATH
MONT. AVE
MIST. CT
STURDEE GRO
STRAYLANDS GROVE
ELMLANDS GROVE
WESTLANDS GROVE
ELMFIELD TER
WILLOW GR
STRAY GARTH
MEADOW WAY
WOODLANDS GROVE
ELMPARK VW
ELMPARK WAY
ELM-PARK VALE
GREENFIELD PARK DRIVE
GREEN SWARD
GREEN MEADOWS
LAWN-WAY
HIGH OAKS
THE GLADE
ASHLEY PARK ROAD
CEDAR GROVE
ALGARTH RD
STOCKTON LANE
CHARLES MOOR
MONK AVE
HERBERT WAY
OAKL. DRIVE
HEMPLAND LANE
HEMP. DR
LIME AVENUE
CHESTNUT AVE
WHITBY AVE
APPLECROFT ROAD
HAZEL GARTH
ASH CL
Allotments
Playing Field
Prim Sch
A1625
A1053
18
19
WARWICK ST
DIAM. ST
NEW LANE
BRECKS LANE
WOODLAND WAY
BRACKEN CL
FERN CL
HEATH. CL
GREENACRES
WOOD WAY
LEA WAY
MEAD. WAY
GREEN WAY
MOOR WAY
KEITH AVENUE
GARTH RD
Prim Sch
PEAR TREE CL
MILL HILL DRIVE
PEN CL
NORTH MOOR
N. MOOR GDNS
MOOR ROAD
YO32
Works
JOCKEY LANE
SADDLERS CLOSE
FORGE CLOSE
F1 Racing
Water World
Sports Centre
KATHRYN AVE
RYEDALE STADIUM
MONKS CROSS DRIVE
Monks Cross Shopping Park
Cem
Thornfield Farm
PASTURE LA
1
2
3
4
5
6
14

14
White Horse Farm
A
9
B
C
D
A64
YORK OUTER RING ROAD
A1237
MALTON ROAD
Beechwood Grange Stud Farm
HUNTINGTON
1
MONKS CROSS LINK
YO32
2
HOPGROVE LANE NORTH
A1036
HOPGROVE LANE
BRANDON GRO
WHEELDALE DRIVE
SOUTH
PO
Monks Cross Shopping Park
MONKS CROSS DRIVE
Hopgrove Playing Fields
Stockton on Forest Inn
F1 Racing
Water Works
3
JULIA AVE
KATHRYN
Sports Centre
ROAD
MALTON
13
Rookstock
Westfield Farm
JOCKEY LANE
LANE
Rowe's Cottage Farm
Beckfield House
4
STOCKTON
Ivy House Farm
Ryethorpe Grange Farm
Cow Moor Farm
A1036
YORK BYPASS
Playing Fields
Lynden Lea
5
Sugar Hill Farm
PASTURE LA
RYCROFT CL
WAY
GREEN SWARD
GREENFIELD PARK
GREEN MEADOWS
BEANS WAY
HILL VIEW
LAWNWAY
DRIVE
HIGH OAKS
GALTRES AVENUE
GALTRES ROAD
LARCHFIELD
Tang Hall Beck
ASHLEY PARK ROAD
THE GLADE
LANE
ALGARTH RD
ALGARTH ROAD
ALGARTH RISE
CEDAR GROVE
YO31
6
CAED CL
SPRINGFIELD WAY
SPR. CL
A64
WHIT. DR
ASH CL
PARK CRES
APPLECROFT ROAD
1453
A
19
Apple Tree Farm
B
C
D
LANE
Allotments
Playing Field
1625
Prim Sch
BRAMLEY
2

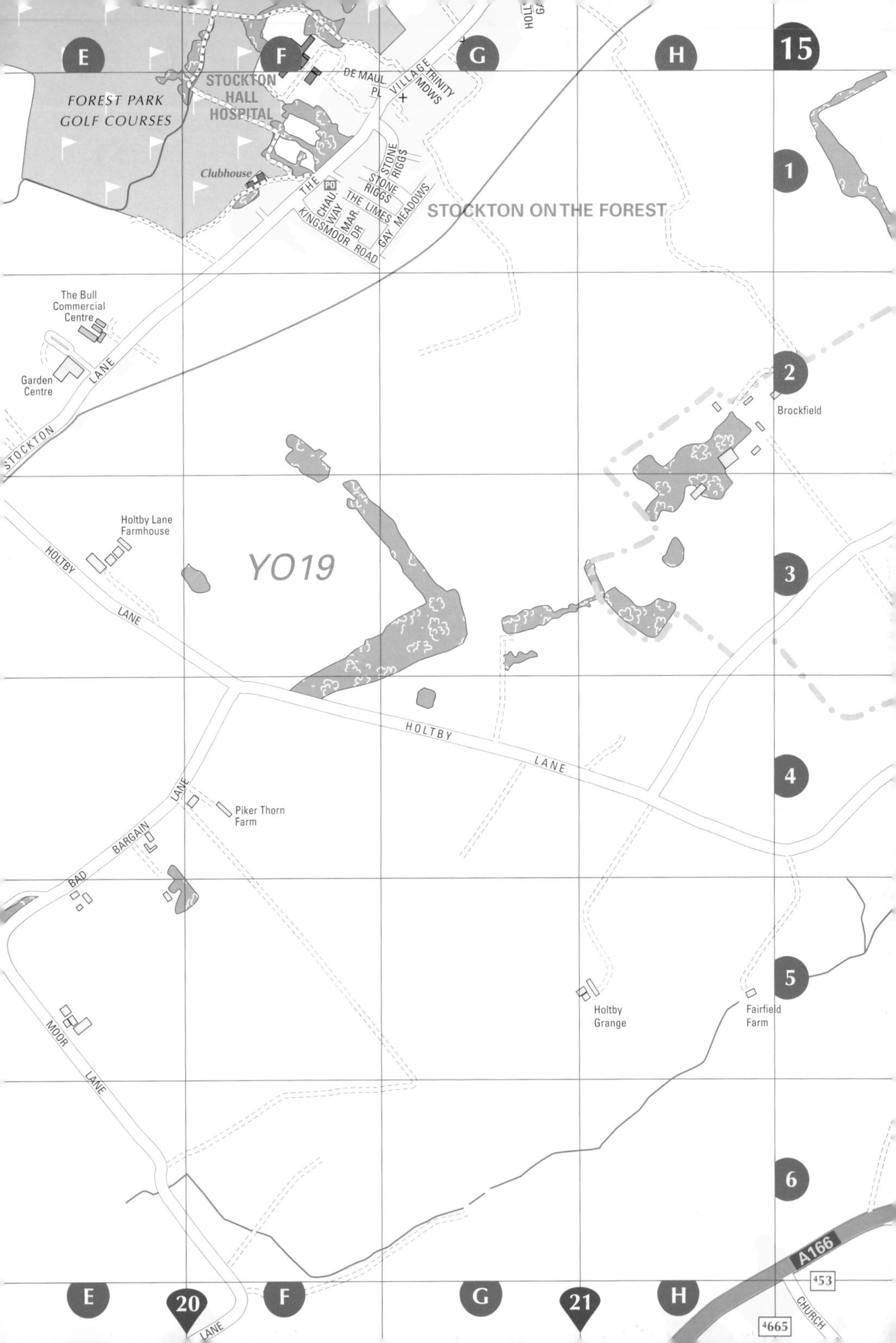
15
E
F
G
H
FOREST PARK
GOLF COURSES
STOCKTON
HALL
HOSPITAL
Clubhouse
DE MAUL PL
VILLAGE
TRINITY MDWS
THE
PO
STONE RIGGS
STONE RIGGS
CHAU. WAY
THE LIMES
MAR. DR
KINGSMOOR ROAD
GAY MEADOWS
STOCKTON ON THE FOREST
1
2
3
4
5
6
The Bull
Commercial
Centre
Garden
Centre
STOCKTON
LANE
Brockfield
Holtby Lane
Farmhouse
HOLTBY
LANE
YO19
HOLTBY
LANE
LANE
BARGAIN
BAD
Piker Thorn
Farm
Holtby
Grange
Fairfield
Farm
MOOR
LANE
A166
453
CHURCH
4665
20
21
LANE

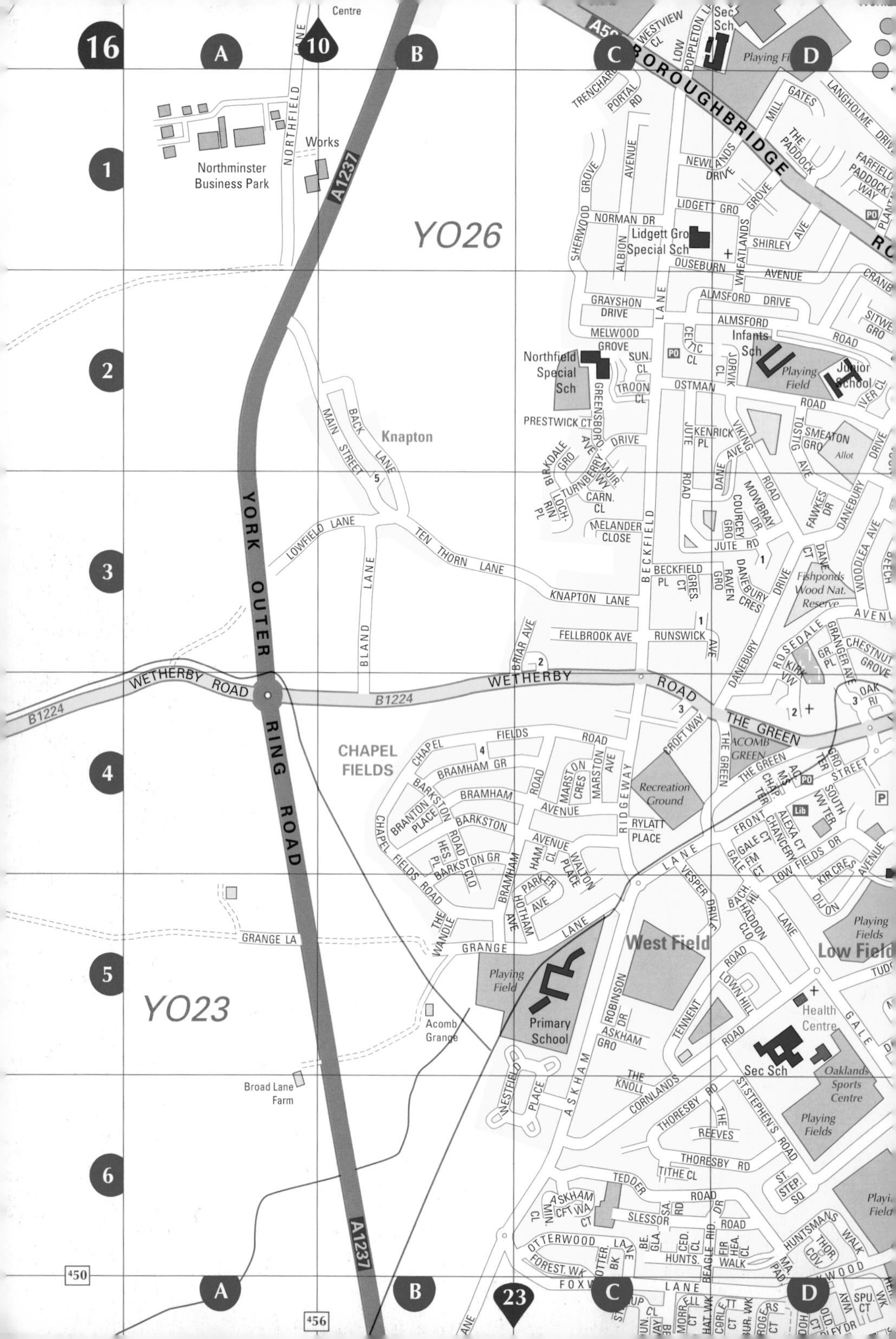
A
B
C
D
1
2
3
4
5
6
10
23
Centre
Works
Northminster
Business Park
NORTHFIELD LANE
A1237
YO26
YO23
YORK OUTER RING ROAD
Knapton
BACK LANE
MAIN STREET
LOWFIELD LANE
TEN THORN LANE
BLAND LANE
KNAPTON LANE
FELLBROOK AVE
BRIAR AVE
WETHERBY ROAD
B1224
CHAPEL FIELDS
CHAPEL FIELDS ROAD
BRAMHAM GR
BRAMHAM AVENUE
BRAMHAM ROAD
BARKSTON PLACE
BARKSTON AVENUE
BARKSTON GR
BRANTON PLACE
MARSTON CRES
MARSTON AVE
RIDGEWAY
RYLATT PLACE
Recreation Ground
HOTHAM AVE
PARKER AVE
WALTON PLACE
THE WANDLE
GRANGE LANE
GRANGE LA
Playing Field
Primary School
West Field
Acomb Grange
Broad Lane Farm
ASKHAM LANE
ASKHAM GRO
ROBINSON DR
WESTFIELD PLACE
THE KNOLL
CORNLANDS ROAD
THORESBY RD
THE REEVES
ST. STEPHEN'S ROAD
TITHE CL
TEDDER ROAD
SLESSOR ROAD
OTTERWOOD LANE
FOREST WK
FOXWOOD LANE
HUNTSMANS WALK
BEAGLE RID. DR
Low Field
Health Centre
Sec Sch
Oaklands Sports Centre
Playing Fields
TENNENT ROAD
LOWN HILL
BACH. HADDON CLO
VESPER DRIVE
LOW FIELDS DR
FRONT STREET
THE GREEN
ACOMB GREEN
CROFT WAY
BECKFIELD LANE
BECKFIELD PL
RUNSWICK AVE
DANEBURY DRIVE
DANEBURY CRES
Fishponds Wood Nat. Reserve
ROSEDALE
KIRK VW
GRANGER AVE
CHESTNUT GROVE
OAK RI
JUTE ROAD
JUTE RD
VIKING ROAD
DANE AVE
MOWBRAY DR
COURCEY GRO
KENRICK PL
OSTMAN ROAD
SMEATON GRO
TOSTIG AVE
FAWKES DR
WOODLEA AVE
Allot
Junior School
Infants Sch
Playing Field
ALMSFORD ROAD
ALMSFORD DRIVE
OUSEBURN AVENUE
WHEATLANDS GROVE
SHIRLEY AVE
LIDGETT GRO
Lidgett Gro Special Sch
NEWLANDS DRIVE
NORMAN DR
ALBION AVENUE
SHERWOOD GROVE
GRAYSHON DRIVE
MELWOOD GROVE
Northfield Special Sch
SUN. CL
TROON CL
GREENSBORO. AVE
PRESTWICK CT
BIRKDALE GRO
TURNBERRY DRIVE
CARN. CL
MELANDER CLOSE
CELTIC CL
JORVIK CL
TRENCHARD RD
PORTAL RD
WESTVIEW CL
LOW POPPLETON LANE
BOROUGHBRIDGE ROAD
MILL GATES
THE PADDOCK
LANGHOLME DRIVE
FARFIELD
PADDOCK WAY
Playing Fi
Sec Sch
PO
Lib
P

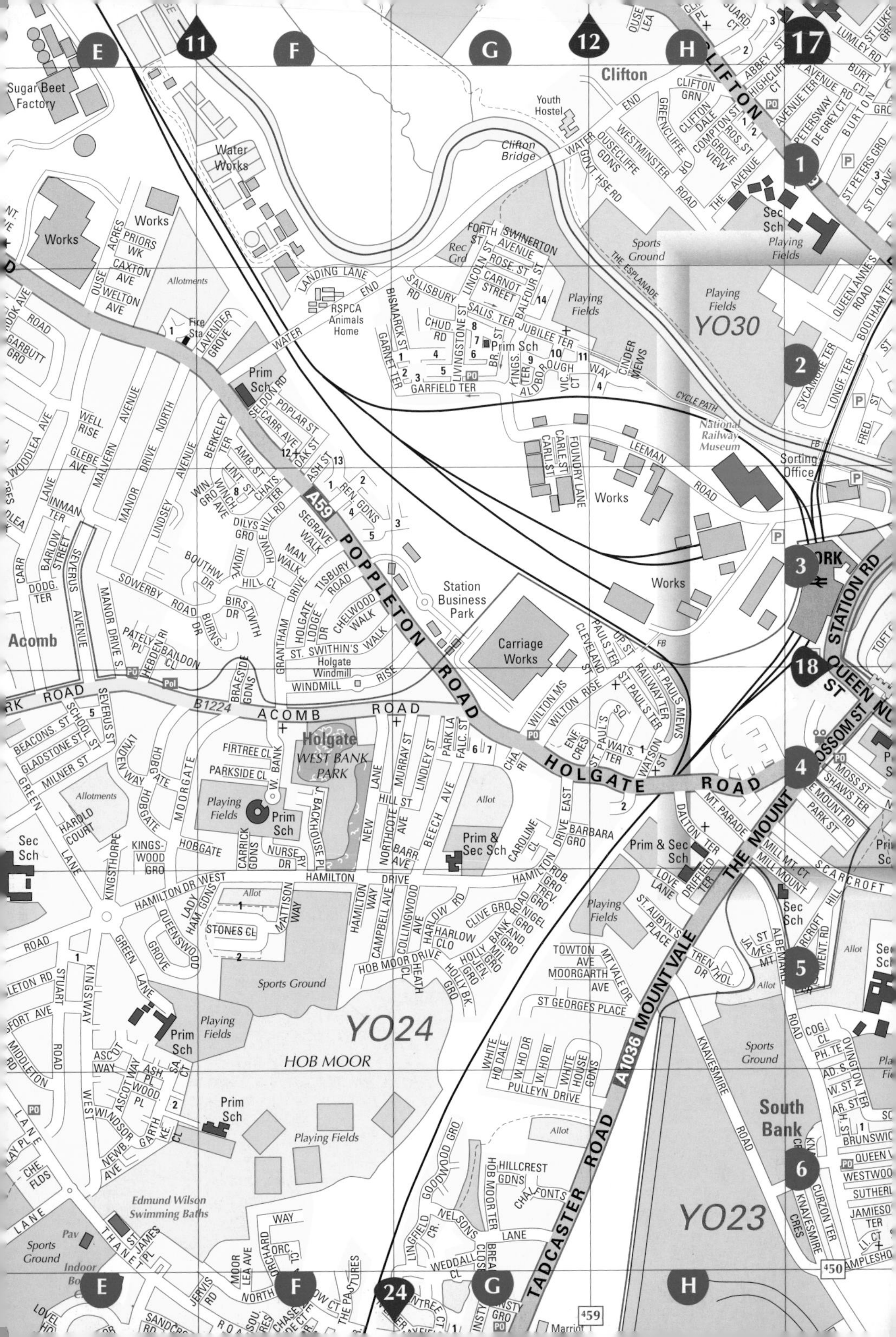
E
F
G
H
11
12
24
18
Clifton
Sugar Beet Factory
Water Works
Works
Youth Hostel
Clifton Bridge
Allotments
Fire Sta
RSPCA Animals Home
Prim Sch
Rec Grd
Sports Ground
Playing Fields
YO30
National Railway Museum
Sorting Office
Works
Station Business Park
Carriage Works
Holgate Windmill
Acomb
Holgate
WEST BANK PARK
Allot
Prim & Sec Sch
Sec Sch
Sports Ground
YO24
HOB MOOR
Playing Fields
Edmund Wilson Swimming Baths
Pav
Indoor
South Bank
YO23
CYCLE PATH
FB
THE ESPLANADE
WATER END
LANDING LANE
POPPLETON ROAD
A59
HOLGATE ROAD
ACOMB ROAD
B1224
THE MOUNT
MOUNT VALE
A1036
TADCASTER ROAD
STATION RD
LEEMAN ROAD
KNAVESMIRE ROAD
HAMILTON DRIVE
HOB MOOR DRIVE
PULLEYN DRIVE
ST GEORGES PLACE
WESTMINSTER ROAD
CLIFTON
BURTON
SCARCROFT
459
450

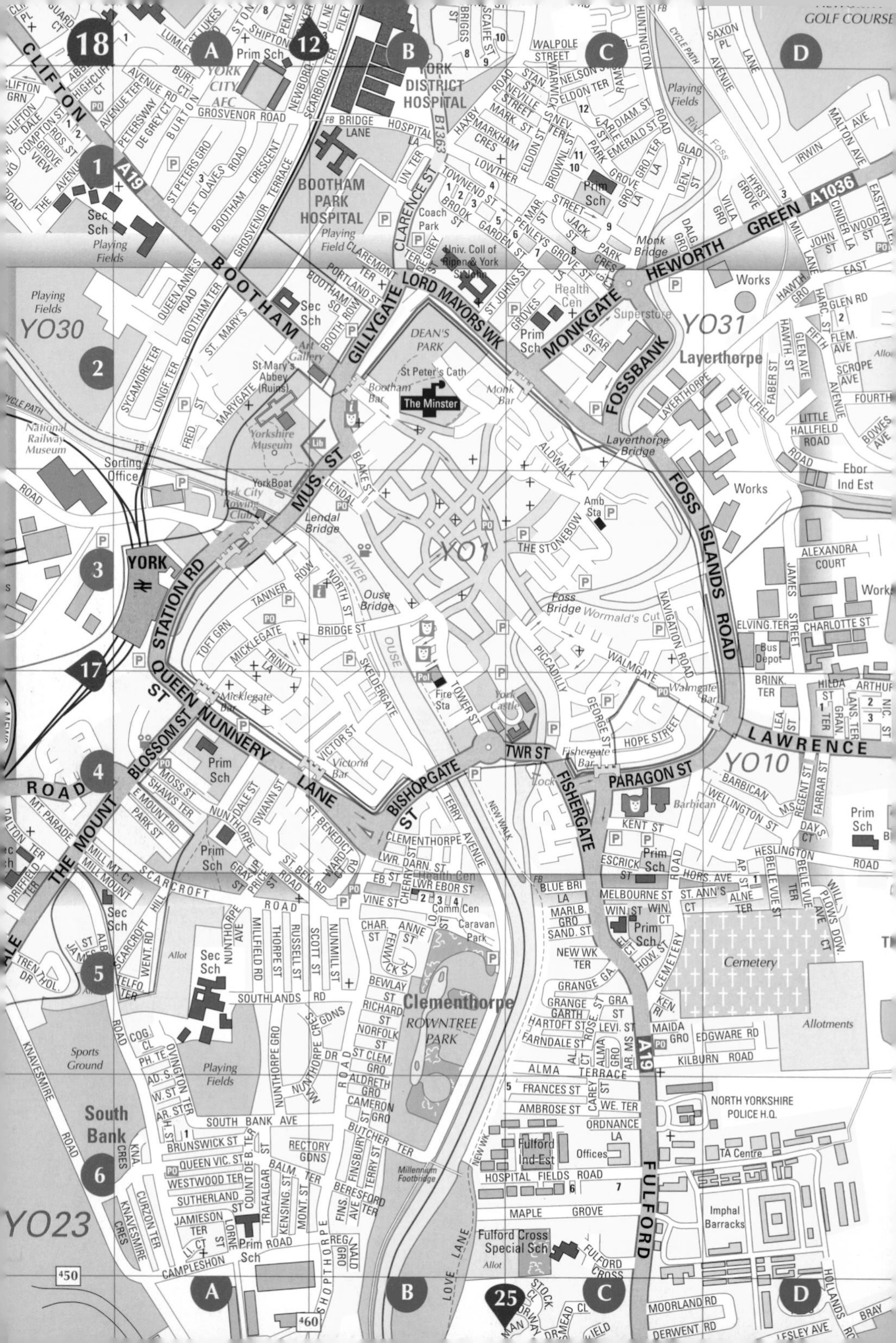
18
12
17
25
A
B
C
D
1
2
3
4
5
6
GOLF COURSE
CLIFTON
YORK CITY AFC
Prim Sch
YORK DISTRICT HOSPITAL
GROSVENOR ROAD
BRIDGE LANE
HOSPITAL LA
WALPOLE STREET
HUNTINGTON ROAD
SAXON PL
LANE AVENUE
Playing Fields
River Foss
MALTON AVE
IRWIN AVE
BOOTHAM PARK HOSPITAL
BOOTHAM CRESCENT
BOOTHAM TERRACE
ST OLAVES ROAD
ST PETERS GRO
A19
Sec Sch
Playing Field
Coach Park
Univ. Coll of Ripon & York St John
LOWTHER
HEWORTH GREEN
A1036
Monk Bridge
Works
YO31
YO30
YO10
YO23
YO1
BOOTHAM
GILLYGATE
LORD MAYORS WK
MONKGATE
FOSSBANK
Superstore
Health Cen
DEAN'S PARK
St Peter's Cath
The Minster
Bootham Bar
Monk Bar
St Mary's Abbey (Ruins)
Art Gallery
Yorkshire Museum
Lib
National Railway Museum
Sorting Office
YorkBoat
York City Rowing Club
MUS. ST
Lendal Bridge
Layerthorpe
Layerthorpe Bridge
FOSS ISLANDS ROAD
Ebor Ind Est
ALEXANDRA COURT
Amb Sta
THE STONEBOW
ALDWALK
Foss Bridge
Wormald's Cut
YORK
STATION RD
QUEEN ST
RIVER OUSE
Ouse Bridge
MICKLEGATE
BRIDGE ST
SKELDERGATE
NORTH ST
TOFT GRN
TANNER ROW
Micklegate Bar
NUNNERY LANE
BLOSSOM ST
Victoria Bar
BISHOPGATE ST
TWR ST
TOWER ST
Fire Sta
Pol
York Castle
PICCADILLY
WALMGATE
Walmgate Bar
GEORGE ST
HOPE STREET
Fishergate Bar
FISHERGATE
PARAGON ST
Barbican
LAWRENCE
Bus Depot
CHARLOTTE ST
JAMES STREET
Works
HESLINGTON ROAD
Cemetery
Allotments
ROAD
THE MOUNT
SCARCROFT ROAD
MOUNT PARADE
CLEMENTHORPE
TERRY AVENUE
NEW WALK
Comm Cen
Caravan Park
Clementhorpe
ROWNTREE PARK
Millennium Footbridge
SOUTHLANDS RD
NUNTHORPE AVE
MILLFIELD RD
THORPE ST
RUSSELL ST
SCOTT ST
NUNMILL ST
Sports Ground
KNAVESMIRE ROAD
South Bank
SOUTH BANK AVE
BRUNSWICK ST
QUEEN VIC. ST
WESTWOOD TER
SUTHERLAND ST
JAMIESON TER
CAMPLESHON ROAD
SHOPTHORPE
RECTORY GDNS
BUTCHER TER
LOVE LANE
Fulford Ind Est
HOSPITAL FIELDS ROAD
MAPLE GROVE
Fulford Cross Special Sch
FULFORD CROSS
FULFORD
ALMA TERRACE
KILBURN ROAD
EDGWARE RD
MAIDA GRO
NORTH YORKSHIRE POLICE H.Q.
TA Centre
Imphal Barracks
Offices
ORDNANCE LA
MOORLAND RD
DERWENT RD
HOLLANDS
450
460

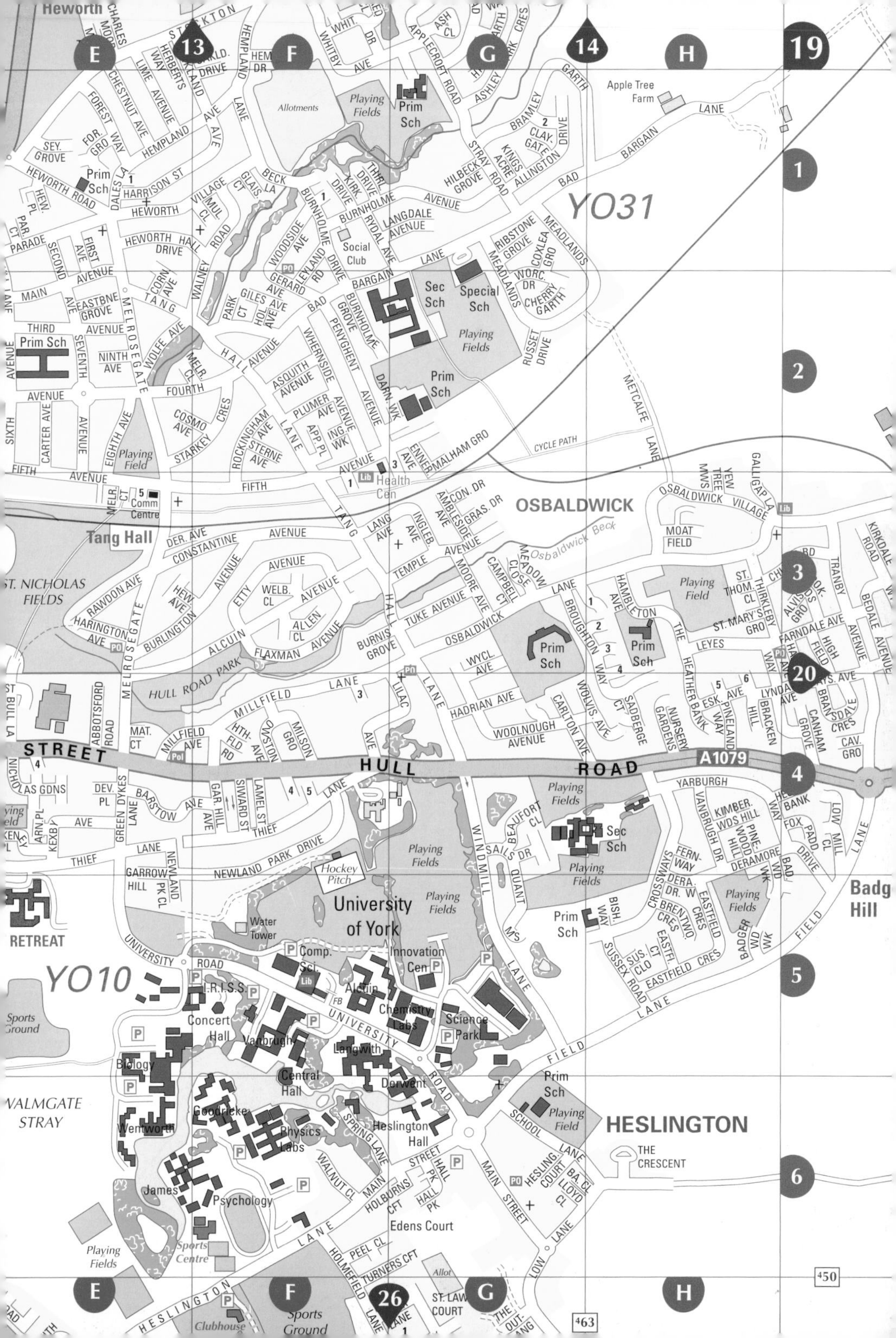

Heworth
13
14
19
20
26
E
F
G
H
1
2
3
4
5
6
YO31
YO10
OSBALDWICK
HESLINGTON
Tang Hall
ST. NICHOLAS FIELDS
HULL ROAD PARK
HULL ROAD
STREET
A1079
University of York
RETREAT
WALMGATE STRAY
Badg Hill
Apple Tree Farm
BARGAIN LANE
BAD BARGAIN LANE
STOCKTON LANE
HEWORTH ROAD
HEWORTH HALL DRIVE
HEWORTH VILLAGE
HEMPLAND LANE
HEMPLAND AVE
APPLECROFT ROAD
STRAY ROAD
HILBECK GROVE
BURNHOLME AVENUE
BURNHOLME DRIVE
BURNHOLME GROVE
LANGDALE AVENUE
WALNEY ROAD
MELROSEGATE
TANG HALL LANE
FIFTH AVENUE
FOURTH AVENUE
SIXTH AVENUE
SEVENTH AVENUE
EIGHTH AVE
NINTH AVE
THIRD AVENUE
SECOND AVENUE
FIRST AVE
CONSTANTINE AVENUE
RAWDON AVE
HARINGTON AVE
BURLINGTON AVENUE
ALCUIN AVENUE
FLAXMAN AVENUE
ETTY AVENUE
TEMPLE AVENUE
TUKE AVENUE
OSBALDWICK LANE
OSBALDWICK VILLAGE
METCALFE LANE
MEADLANDS
RIBSTONE GROVE
RUSSET DRIVE
CYCLE PATH
Osbaldwick Beck
MOAT FIELD
THE LEYES
HEATHER BANK
NURSERY GARDENS
KIRKDALE ROAD
TRANBY AVENUE
BEDALE AVENUE
FARNDALE AVE
MILLFIELD LANE
MILLFIELD AVE
LILAC AVE
HADRIAN AVE
WOOLNOUGH AVENUE
CARLTON AVE
WOLVIS AVE
ABBOTSFORD ROAD
BULL LA
NICHOLAS GDNS
GREEN DYKES LANE
BARSTOW AVE
THIEF LANE
NEWLAND PARK DRIVE
GARROW HILL
WINDMILL LANE
YARBURGH WAY
VANBRUGH DR
DERAMORE DRIVE
EASTFIELD CRES
SUSSEX ROAD
BADGER WD WK
FIELD LANE
UNIVERSITY ROAD
HESLINGTON LANE
MAIN STREET
SCHOOL LANE
HOLMEFIELD LANE
LOW LANE
THE CRESCENT
Edens Court
ST. LAW COURT
THE OUT-GANG
Prim Sch
Sec Sch
Special Sch
Playing Fields
Playing Field
Allotments
Social Club
Health Cen
Comm Centre
Hockey Pitch
Water Tower
Comp. Sci.
Innovation Cen
I.R.I.S.S.
Alcuin
Chemistry Labs
Science Park
Concert Hall
Vanbrugh
Langwith
Biology
Central Hall
Derwent
Goodricke
Wentworth
Physics Labs
Heslington Hall
James
Psychology
Sports Centre
Sports Ground
Clubhouse
Allot
450
463

A
14
B
C
D
LANE
1
Murton
MOOR LANE
The Bay Horse (PH)
MURTON GARTH
MURTON
YORK
SMARY LANE
WAY
BYPASS
Derwent Valley Light Railway
2
MURTON
Yorkshire Museum of Farming
Murton Park
LANE
FRYERS CT
OUTGANG LANE
Depot
York Livestock Centre
A64
GALLIGAP LA
YEW TREE MWS
OSBALDWICK VILLAGE
Lib
STAMFORD
KIRKDALE ROAD
OSBALDWICK LINK ROAD
WENSLEYDALE DR
TRANBY
BROOKLANDS
Playing Field
3
ST. THOM. CL
KIRKLEBY GRO
ALVIS GRO
A166
BEDALE AVENUE
WYDALE RD
ST. MARY'S GRO
FARNDALE AVE
HIGH FIELD
AVENUE
A1079
LEYES
HEATHER BANK
PO
HAZEL AVE
The Oaks
19
BAYS. AVE
ROAD
ELVINGTON LANE
Lodge Farm
ESK. AVE
PINELAND WAY
HILL
BRACKEN
CANHAM GROVE
BRANSDALE CRES
Retail Park
Grimston Bar
A1079
CAV. GRO
HULL
4
YARBURGH
HESKETH BANK
VANBRUGH DR
KIMBER. WDS HILL
PINEWOOD HILL
WAY
FOX PADD.
LOW MILL CL
LANE
FERN-WAY
DERAMORE DRIVE
BAD. WD WK
Badger Hill
Playing Fields
EASTFIELD CRES
BADGER WD WK
FIELD
YORK BYPASS
YO10
ELD CRES
5
NGTON
6
A64
Grimston Grange
450
A
B
27
C
D
464

E
15
F
A166
G
H
1
2
3
4
5
6
CHURCH BALK
EASTFIELD LANE
STOCK-HILL CL
GARDEN FLATS LA
GORSE HILL
HOLLY TREE LA
HOLLY TREE CFT
ASPEN CL
PETERCR. CLOSE
PETERCROFT LANE
KENDAL CLOSE
UNDER-CFT
THORN-CFT
CONEY-CFT
HORSFIELD WAY
KERVER LANE
SAW. WK
TWINAM CT
KEEPER'S WAY
SPRING BK AVE
CHURCH LA
THE COPPER BEECH.
THE MANOR BEECHES
CHURCH STREET
THE GLEBE
Lib
Prim Sch
B. CL
COPPER MANOR DR
CHURCH LANE
HUNT. CL
PEAR TREE LANE
YORK STREET
PO
OWL CT
GREEN. CT
GRNCRFT. LANE
COMMON ROAD
WATER LANE
LIME TR. MEWS
SCAU.-CFT
ASHD. RD
OX CALDER CLOSE
INTAKE LANE
THE GRN
OWLWOOD LANE
CURLEW GLEBE
GREENSIDE
GREENSIDE CL
GREENSIDE WALK
HUNTERS WAY
DEERST. WAY
CEDAR GLADE
DERWENT LANE
DERWENT EST
Allot
DUNNINGTON
Sports Ground
Pavilion
Thorntree Hill Farm
YORK ROAD
BRIDGE ROAD
YO19
Grimstone Court
HULL ROAD
A1079
Chessingham Park
Derwent Valley Estates
HAGG LANE
Farm
B1228
ELVINGTON LANE
Fir Tree Farm
Breckon Farm
Coney Garth Farm
Common Farm
DUNNINGTON COMMON
Church Lane Farm
Clock Farm
450
467

23
A1237
A64
YORK BYPASS
A
B
C
D
1
2
3
4
5
6
YO23
COPMANTHORPE
PIKE HILLS MOUNT
ST. NICHOLAS CRES
ST. NICH. CL
ST. NICHOLAS RD
THE LINK
COLLEGE ROAD
MANOR HEATH
LARK. CL
TOP LANE
MERCHANT WAY
WEAVERS PARK
DRAPERS CFT
COOP. DR
WEAV. CL
BARBE. DR
BOWYERS CL
CROFT
FLAXMAN CROFT
ROPERS CT
LEARMANS WAY
HALLCROFT LANE
HORSEMAN LANE
HORSEMAN AVE
MILL CFT
SUT. CL
FAB. CL
FLAXMAN
GAR. CL
LORIN. DR
WH. CL
FARMERS WAY
PLOU. CL
WHI. CL
HER. DR
SAW.
CRES
RUTLAND CLOSE
LYNWOOD VW
HORSEMAN DR
LYNWOOD AVE
HORSE CLOSE
LYNWOOD CLOSE
ORCHARD GARTH
CFT FM CL
LOW GREEN
Playing Fields
Prim Sch
Rec Centre
Sports Ground
Pol
Lib
SCHOOL LANE
CH ST
BACK LANE
MANOR FM CLOSE
PO
MAIN STREET
STAK. ORCH.
REYGATE GRO
MALBYS GRO
BARONS CRES
VIC. CL
ST. GILES
BELLMANS CFT
FAIRF. CFT
DEACONS CT
BEAD. GARTH
WAY
VAV. CT
WILSTROP FM RD
HOM. CL
BARNFIELD W.
PADD. CL
STATION ROAD
Allot
TEMPLE LANE
DROME ROAD
TEMPLE GARTH
HOB. CL
DYKES LANE
NALT. CL
LEADLEY CFT
MOORLAND GDNS
MOOR LANE
Cem
447
456
WESTWOOD LANE
MAIN STREET
ST. NICHOLAS CFT
SCHOOL LANE
MOW. CT
DE
Prim Sch
PADD. CL
SNOWDON CLOSE
Askham Grange Prison
ASKHAM RICHARD
MAIN STREET
BUT. LA
Askham Fields Farm
Sports Ground
453
Highfield
Inn

For continuation see inset on p22

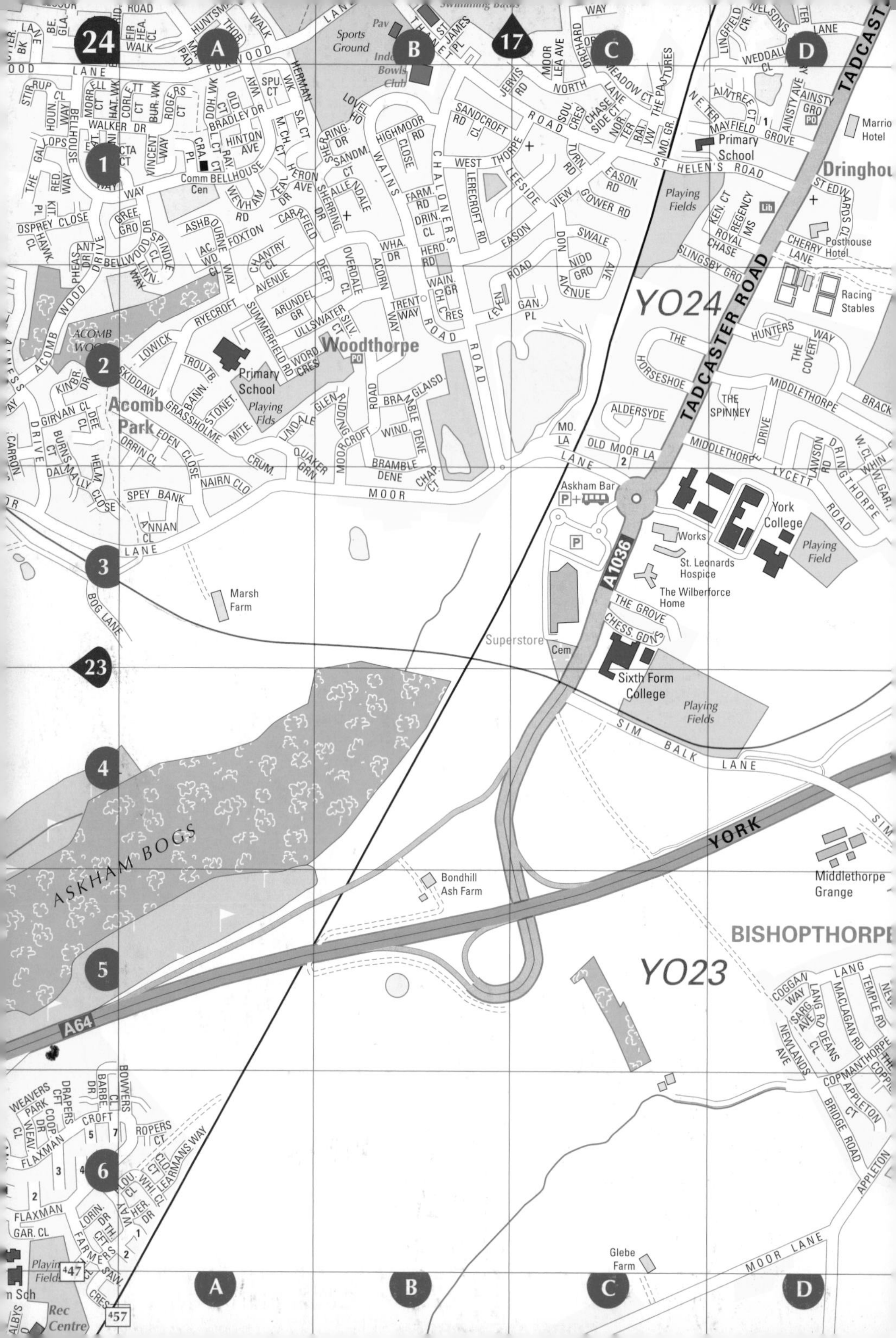
24
17
23
A
B
C
D
1
2
3
4
5
6
Sports Ground
Pav
Indoor Bowls Club
FOXWOOD LANE
HERMAN WK.
WALKER DR
BELLHOUSE WAY
BRADLEY DR
HINTON AVE
VINCENT WAY
Comm Cen
OSPREY CLOSE
ACOMB WOOD DRIVE
ACOMB WOOD
BELLWOOD DR
SPINDLE
FOXTON
ASHBOURNE WAY
CHANTRY AVENUE
RYECROFT
LOWICK
SUMMERFIELD RD
ARUNDEL GR
ULLSWATER
Woodthorpe
PO
Primary School
Playing Flds
Acomb Park
GRASSHOLME
EDEN CLOSE
NAIRN CLO
SPEY BANK
ANNAN CL
MOOR LANE
BOG LANE
Marsh Farm
HIGHMOOR RD
CLOSE
WAINS ROAD
CHALONERS ROAD
SANDCROFT RD
WEST THORPE
LERECROFT RD
LEESIDE
EASON VIEW
GOWER RD
SWALE AVE
NIDD GRO
DON AVENUE
LEVEN ROAD
GAN. PL
NORTH LANE
THE PASTURES
ST HELEN'S ROAD
Playing Fields
Primary School
MAYFIELD GROVE
AINSTY GRO
Marriott Hotel
Dringhouses
REGENCY MS
ROYAL CHASE
SLINGSBY GRO
CHERRY LANE
Posthouse Hotel
Racing Stables
YO24
TADCASTER ROAD
HUNTERS WAY
THE HORSESHOE
THE COVERT
MIDDLETHORPE DRIVE
THE SPINNEY
ALDERSYDE
OLD MOOR LA
BRAMBLE DENE
MOORCROFT
QUAKER GRN
Askham Bar
A1036
Works
St. Leonards Hospice
The Wilberforce Home
York College
Playing Field
LYCETT ROAD
DRINGTHORPE ROAD
THE GROVE
CHESS. GDNS
Superstore
Cem
Sixth Form College
Playing Fields
SIM BALK LANE
ASKHAM BOGS
YORK
A64
Bondhill Ash Farm
Middlethorpe Grange
BISHOPTHORPE
YO23
COGGAN WAY
LANG RD
MACLAGAN RD
TEMPLE RD
NEWLANDS AVE
COPMANTHORPE
APPLETON CT
BRIDGE ROAD
APPLETON
MOOR LANE
Glebe Farm
WEAVERS PARK
DRAPERS CFT
CROFT
BOWYERS
ROPERS CT
FLAXMAN
LEARMANS WAY
FARMERS
Playing Fields
Rec Centre
Sch
47
57

YO23
E
F
G
H
18
25
26
1
2
3
4
5
6
Barracks
JAMIESON TER
LORNE ST
LILY CT
CAMP
KNAVESMIRE CRES
Prim Sch
ROAD
REGINALD GRO
BISHOPTHORPE ROAD
LOVE LANE
Fulford Cross Special Sch
Allot
STOCK. CL
NORWAY DR
REDMAN CL
DANE CFT
DANESMEAD CL
WESTFIELD DR
MOORLAND RD
DERWENT RD
LESLEY AV
MOOR. FLDS
BROADWAY
BROADWAY WEST
PO
THE LINK
ANSON DR
ROAD
CORN DR
WEL DR
DANUM DR
END. RD
GRANTS
Playing Field
CROSS. RD
GARTHS END
Caravan Park
ST.OSWALDS ROAD
CONN. CT
ATCHE. CL
ST. AIDANS CT
HESLINGTON
Prim Sch
FULFORD GATE
Residential Homes
FULFORD PARK
Lib
SCHOOL LANE
FENW. LANE
Gate Fulford Hall
ELIOT CT
MAIN STREET
Playing Field
FUL
Fulford Ings
DELWOOD
PROSPECT TER
THE OLD ORC.
PALACE VW
PO
GLEN CL
PASTURE FM CL
FULFORD MEWS
FORDLANDS
FORDLA. CRES
FULFORD ROAD
SELBY ROAD
A19
Hall Farm
Fulford Hall
B1222
A64
MICKLEGATE STRAY
Grandstand
Chocolate Factory
P
York Race Course Car Parks
YORK RACE COURSE
Allotments
Manor Farm
College of Law
Playing Fields
KNAVESMIRE WOOD
Middlethorpe
WOR. PL.
LADY
Middlethorpe Manor
GREEN LANE
Middlethorpe Ings
GREEN LANE
ASS
A64
Crematorium
RIVER OUSE
Fulford Court
A64
BALK
BISHOPTHORPE ROAD
Archbishop of York's Palace
NABURN LANE
McArthurGlen Designer Outlet
ST.NICHOLAS AVE
CHURCH LANE
LANE
Prim School
PO
THE COURT.
MAIN STREET
CHANTRY LANE
Ruin
Lib
SCHOOL LA
CROFT COURT
FERRY LANE
Sports Ground
MAPLE
MONTAGUE ROAD
HARCO. CL
DE GREY PL
VIEW
DRUMMOND
ACASTER
MYRTLE AVE
AVE
VERNON CL
RAMSEY AVE
LANE
CODA AVE
Sports Ground
THE ORCHARD
BEECH
WOLSEY DRIVE
MELTON DRIVE
NEVILLE DRIVE
AVENUE
CRESCENT
LAMPL.
GARB. WAY
Allot
KEB CL.
NORTH
LANE
KEBLE PARK
KEBLE DR
KEBLE PARK SO
KEBLE PK CRES
KEBLE GDNS
ACASTER
Works
Works
B1222
YO19
Naburn Lodge Farm
47
61

26
19
25
A
B
C
D
1
2
3
4
5
6
Barracks
Edens Court
FULFORD ROAD
FULFORD CROSS
MOORLAND RD
DERWENT RD
MOOR FLDS
HOLLANDS ROAD
BRAY ROAD
SMITH CL
LESLEY AVE
BROADWAY
HESLINGTON LANE
PEEL CL
HOLMEFIELD LANE
TURNERS CFT
WEST MOOR LANE
ST. LAWRENCE COURT
Allot
THE OUT-GANG
GARROWBY WAY
LOW LANE
Clubhouse
Sports Ground
PO
THE LINK
DANUM DR
CORN. DR
ROAD WEL
END RD
GRANTS AVE
BARMBY AVE
BROADW. GRO
STIRL. GROVE
WILSTH. GRO
NEVINSON GROVE
HEATH MOOR DRIVE
TILMIRE CLOSE
Playing Field
CROSS. RD
GARTHS END
ST. AIDANS CT
HESLINGTON
HESL. CFT
HEATH CROFT
LOW MOOR AVE
FULFORD PARK
Prim Sch
FULFORD-GATE
EASTWARD AVENUE
Lib
SCHOOL LANE
Sec Sch
FULFORD GOLF COURSE
Gate Fulford Hall
FENW. LANE
THE OLD ORC.
FULFORD
DELWOOD
PROSPECT TER
PALACE VW
PASTURE FM CL
GLEN CL
MAIN STREET
FULFORD MEWS
FORDLANDS ROAD
Cemetery
YO19
CROSSFIELD CRES
FORDLA. CRES
EAST GDNS
KEY WAY
CROSS LANE
CHERRY WOOD CRES
Hall Farm
SELBY ROAD
B1222
A19
A64
YORK
Lodge Farm
McArthurGlen Designer Outlet
ST. NICHOLAS AVE
Offices
Forest Farm
Tilmire Farm
Lingcroft Farm
447
461

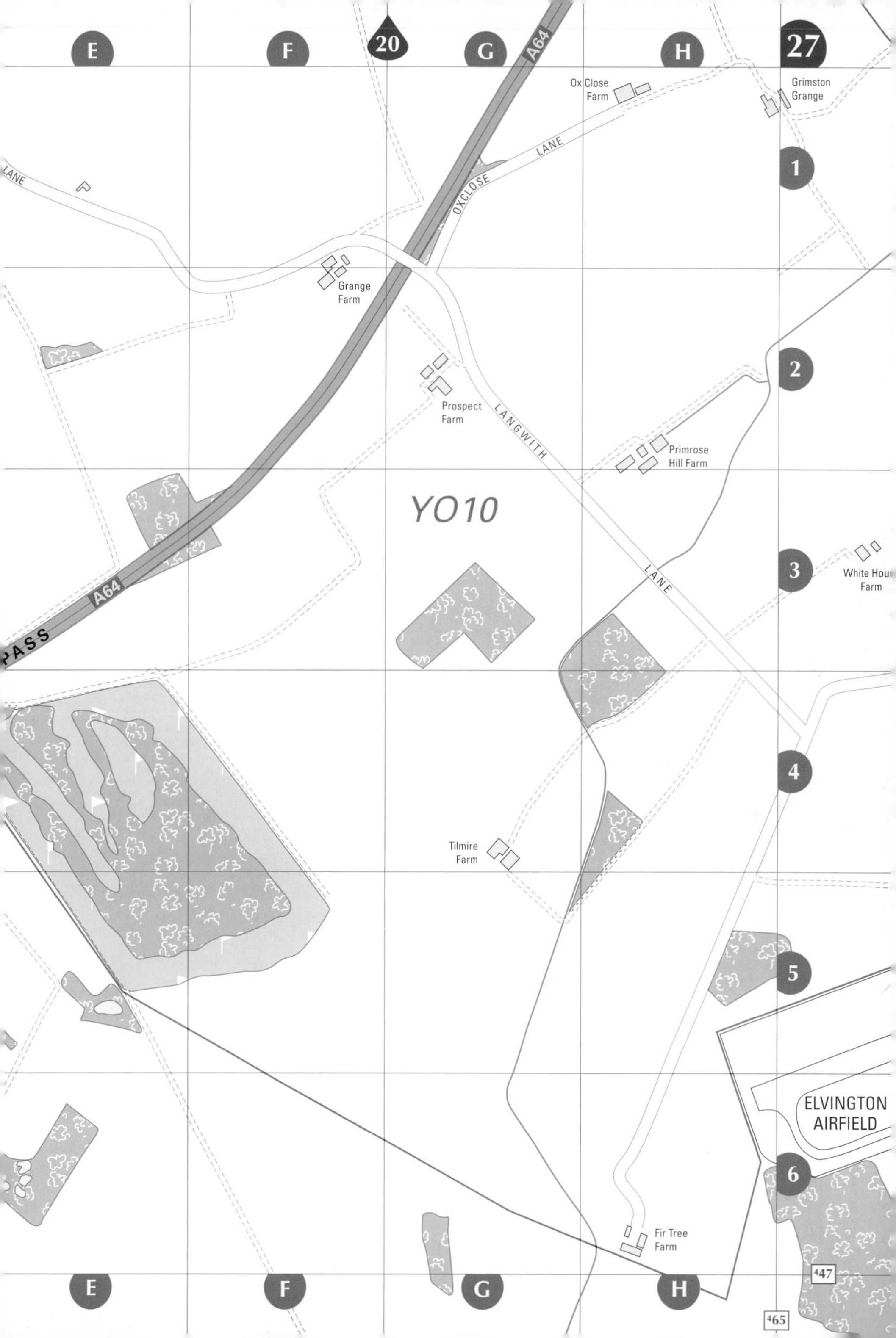
E
F
20
G
H
A64
Ox Close Farm
Grimston Grange
LANE
OXCLOSE LANE
Grange Farm
Prospect Farm
LANGWITH
Primrose Hill Farm
YO10
LANE
White Hous Farm
PASS
A64
Tilmire Farm
ELVINGTON AIRFIELD
Fir Tree Farm
1
2
3
4
5
6
447
465
E
F
G
H

USEFUL INFORMATION

Crematorium
Bishopthorpe Road, Middlethorpe YO23 2QD
Tel: 01904 706096 **25 F4**

Central Library
Library Square, Museum Street YO1 7DS
Tel: 01904 655631 **4 D2**

Main Post Office
22 Lendal YO1 8DA *Tel: 01904 617210* **4 D3**

North Yorkshire Police
Headquarters, Fulford Road YO10 4BY
Tel: 01904 631321 **18 C6**

Lower Friargate YO1 9SL *Tel: 01904 669501* **5 E5**

Acomb Road, Acomb YO24 4HA *Tel: 01904 669550* **17 E3**

Stirling Road, Clifton Moor YO30 4WZ
Tel: 01904 669403 **12 B1**

Tourist Information
De Grey Rooms, Exhibition Square YO1 7HB
Tel: 01904 621756 Web Site: www.york-tourism.co.uk **4 D2**

ADMINISTRATION

City of York Council *Web Site: www.york.gov.uk*
The Guildhall YO1 9QN
Tel: 01904 613161 **4 D3**

Commercial Services Department
Foss Islands Depot, Foss Islands Road YO31 7ZR
Tel: 01904 625751 **5 G3**

Community Services, Customer Advice Centre
10-12 George Hudson Street YO1 6ZE
Tel: 01904 613161 **4 C4**

Educational Services
Mill House, North Street YO1 7ZR
Tel: 01904 613161 **4 D4**

Environment and Development Services
9 St Leonard's Place YO1 7ET
Tel: 01904 613161 **4 D2**

Leisure Services
18 Back Swinegate, Swinegate Court YO1 8ZD
Tel: 01904 613161 **5 E3**

Resources Group
City Finance Centre, Library Square YO1 7DU
Tel: 01904 613161 **4 D2**

ENTERTAINMENT

Cinemas
City Screen, Coney Street YO1 9QL
Tel: 01904 541144/541155
Web Site: www.picturehouse-cinemas.co.uk/yk **4 D3**

Odeon Cinema, Blossom Street YO24 1AJ
Tel: 01904 623287 Web Site: www.odeon.co.uk **4 B5**

Warner Village, Stirling Road, Clifton Moor YO30 4XY
Tel: 01904 691094/691199
Web Site: www.warnervillage.co.uk **12 A2**

Theatres
Barbican Centre, Paragon Street YO10 4NT
Tel: 01904 628991 Booking Office 01904 656688
Web Site: www.fibbers.co.uk/barbican **5 G6**

De Grey Rooms, Exhibition Square YO1 7HB
Tel: 01904 613161 **4 D2**

Friargate Theatre, Lower Friargate YO1 9SL
Tel: 01904 613000 Web Site: www.ridinglights.org **5 E4**

Grand Opera House, 4 Cumberland Street YO1 9SW
Tel: 01904 655441 Booking Office 01904 671818
Web Site: www.york-operahouse.co.uk **5 E4**

Joseph Rowntree Theatre, Haxby Road YO31 8XY
Tel: 01904 602440 **13 E5**

Theatre Royal, St.Leonards Place YO1 7HD
Tel: 01904 623568/610041
Web Site: www.theatre-royal-york.co.uk **4 D2**

FURTHER EDUCATION

Askham Bryan College, Askham Bryan YO23 3FR
Tel: 01904 772277
Web Site: www.askham-bryan.ac.uk **23 E6**

The College of Law, Bishopthorpe Road Y023 2GA
Tel: 0800 318130
Web Site: www.lawcol.org.uk/cliyork1.html **25 F3**

University College of Ripon and York St John,
Lord Mayor's Walk YO31 7EX
Tel: 01904 656771 Web Site: www.ucrysj.ac.uk **5 E1**

University of York, Heslington YO10 5DD
Tel: 01904 430000 Web Site: www.york.ac.uk **19 F5**

York College, Tadcaster Road, Dringhouses YO24 1UA
Tel: 01904 770200
Web Site: www.yorkcollege.com **24 D3**

HEALTH

York Health NHS Trust
Bootham Park Hospital, Bootham YO30 7BY
Tel: 01904 610777 **18 B1**

York District Hospital, Wiggington Road YO31 7HE
Tel: 01904 631313 A & E Department **12 D6**

Tees, East and N Yorkshire Ambulance Service NHS Trust
Ambulance Headquarters, Fairfields, Shipton Road
YO30 1XW *Tel: 01904 666000* **11 E1**

Independent Hospitals
Pury Cust Nuffield Hospital, Precentor's Court YO1 7EL
Tel: 01904 641571
Web Site: www.nuffieldhospitals.org.uk **4 D2**

Stockton Hall Hospital, The Village, Stockton on the Forest
YO32 9UN *Tel: 01904 400500* **15 F1**

The Retreat, 107 Heslington Road YO10 5BN
Tel: 01904 412551
Web Site: www.retreat-hospital.org **19 E5**

HELP AND ADVICE

Citizens Advice Bureau,
3 Blossom Street YO24 1AU
Tel: 01904 636066
Web Site: www.nacab.org.uk **4 C5**

Samaritans, 89 Nunnery Lane YO23 1AH
Tel: 01904 655888 Web Site: www.samaritans.org.uk **4 C5**

Victim Support, 10 Priory Street YO1 6EX
Tel: 01904 636905
Web Site: www.victimsupport.com **4 C5**

National Helplines

Missing Persons *Tel: 0500 700 700*
Web Site: www.missingpersons.org

Childline *Tel: 0800 1111*
Web Site: www.childline.org.uk

NSPCC Child Protection *Tel: 0800 800500*
Web Site: www.nspcc.org.uk

Rape Crisis Federation *Tel: 0115 934 8474*
Web Site: www.rapecrisis.co.uk

RSPCA *Tel: 0870 444 3127 Web Site: www.rspca.org.uk*

MEDIA

Local Newspapers

York Advertiser (weekly) *Tel: 01904 639136*

York Star (weekly) *Tel: 01904 653051*

Yorkshire Evening Post (daily) *Tel: 0113 243 2701*

Yorkshire Evening Press (daily) *Tel: 01904 611488*

Yorkshire Gazette & Herald (weekly) *Tel: 01904 611488*

Yorkshire Post (daily) *Tel: 0113 243 2701*

Local Radio

Minster FM FM104.7 MHz
Tel: 01904 488888 Web Site: www.minsterfm.com

BBC Radio York FM 95.5,103.7,104.3 MHz
Tel: 01904 641351
Web Site:www.bbc.co.uk/england/radioyork

SPORT & LEISURE

Association Football

York City F.C., Bootham Crescent YO30 7AQ
Tel: 01904 624447 Web Site: www.ycfc.net **18 A1**

Golf

Fulford Golf Club, Heslington Lane, Heslington
YO10 5DY *Tel: 01904 413579* **26 C1**

Forest of Galtres Golf Club, Skelton Lane, Wigginton
YO32 3RF *Tel: 01904 766198* **6 C3**

Heworth Golf Club, Muncaster House, Muncastergate
YO31 9JY *Tel: 01904 422389* **13 G6**

Pike Hills Golf Club, Tadcaster Road YO23 3UW
Tel: 01904 700797 **23 G5**

Horse Racing

York Racecourse YO23 1EX *Tel: 01904 620911* **25 F1**

Motor Racing

F1 Racing Premier Karting, Monks Cross YO32 9JF
Tel: 01904 673555 Web Site: www.karting.uk.com **13 H3**

Rugby League

York Wasps, Ryedale Stadium, Kathryn Avenue,
Huntington YO32 9JS *Tel: 01904 634636* **13 H3**

Sports & Leisure Centres/Swimming Pools

Barbican Centre, Barbican Road YO1 4NT
Tel: 01904 630266 **5 G6**

Edmund Wilson Swimming Pool, Thanet Road, Acomb
YO24 2NW *Tel: 01904 793031* **17 E6**

Ryedale Stadium, Kathryn Avenue, Huntington YO32 9JS
Tel: 01904 642111 **13 H3**

Oaklands Sports Centre, Cornlands Road, Acomb
YO24 3DX *Tel: 01904 782841* **16 D5**

Water World, Kathryn Avenue, Monk's Cross YO32 9JS
Tel: 01904 642111 **13 H3**

Yearsley Swimming Pool, Haley's Terrace, Haxby Road
YO31 8SB *Tel: 01904 622773* **13 E5**

Shopping

Shopmobility, Piccadilly Car Park *Tel: 01904 679222*
Web Site: www.disabilityuk.com **5 E4**

Clifton Moor, Stirling Road YO30 4XZ
Tel: 01904 690206 **12 A2**

Coppergate Centre, Coppergate YO1 9NT
Tel: 01904 627160 **4 E4**

McArthurglen Designer Outlet, St Nicholas Ave, Fulford
YO19 4TA *Tel: 01904 682700*
Web Site: www.mcarthurglen-york.co.uk **25 H5**

Monks Cross Shopping Park, Monks Cross Drive,
Huntington YO32 9GX *Tel: 01904 623374*
Web Site: www.monkscross.net **14 A2**

Newgate Market YO1 7LA *(open 7 days a week)*
Tel: 01904 551355 **5 E3**

Bookshops

Blackwells, University of York, Heslington YO10 5DU
Tel: 01904 432715 Web Site: www.blackwells.co.uk **19 F5**

Borders Books and Music, 1/5 Davygate YO1 8QY
Tel: 01904 653300 Web Site: www.bordersstores.com **4 D3**

Waterstone's *Web Site: www.waterstones.co.uk*
28/29 High Ousegate YO1 2RX *Tel: 01904 628740* **5 E4**
9/10 High Ousegate YO1 2RZ *Tel: 01904 653300* **5 E4**

W.H.Smith *Web Site: www.whsmith.co.uk*
39/41 Coney Street YO1 9QL *Tel: 01904 623106* **4 D3**
Monks Cross Shopping Park YO32 9GX
Tel: 01904 622555 **14 A2**

TRANSPORT

Bus Services

BusInfo Centre, 20 George Hudson Street YO1 6WR
Tel: 01904 551400 **4 C4**

Dial and Ride *Tel: 01904 624455*
York Wheels *Tel: 01904 630080*

Coach Parks

St. Johns, Clarence Street YO31 **18 B1**
Kent Street YO10 **5G6**

Lorry Park

St. Johns, Clarence Street YO31 **18 B1**

Park & Ride

Askham Bar *Tel: 01904 707726* **24 C3**

Rawcliffe Bar *Tel: 01904 541333* **11 G3**

Grimston Bar *Tel: 01904 431388* **20 B4**

McArthurglen Designer Outlet (Mon to Fri)
Tel: 01904 435637 **25 H5**

Rail

Railway Station, Station Road YO24 1AB **4 B4**
National Rail Enquiries *Tel: 08457 484950*
Web Site: www.railtrack.co.uk

Places of Interest

☐ Indicates a place of interest that appears in the street map pages. An explanation of the other symbols can be found on page 35.

Abbey House Museum 36 A5
The museum, housed partly in the gatehouse of the 12c church at Kirkstall, includes reconstructed Victorian streets with houses, shops and workshops furnished with period artefacts and exhibitions about the social history of Leeds and Kirkstall Abbey.

Allerton Park 36 C3
A 19c mansion in a large park with lakes, to the north east of Knaresborough.

☐ **ARC** 5 F3
A hands-on archaeology resource centre in the medieval church of St. Saviour in York city centre. There are opportunities to sort and date authentic finds, plan an excavation using computers, and try the ancient crafts of spinning and weaving.

☐ **Barley Hall** 5 E2
The medieval oak-framed home of Alderman Snawsell restored to how it would have been in the 1480's using authentic materials and techniques. Located off Stonegate in the heart of York.

Battle of Boroughbridge 1322 36 C2
A battle site, where the rebellious Earl of Lancaster was defeated and executed by his cousin, Edward II, after hostilities broke out.

Battle of Marston Moor 1644 36 C3
The scene of the largest battle of this Civil War. The Royalists, led by Prince Rupert, were defeated by the Parliamentarians and lost control of the North.

Battle of Myton 1319 36 C2
The battle site where Edward II was defeated by the Scots during Scottish Wars of Independence. Rare documentation from the time shows military tactics used in this period.

Battle of Stamford Bridge 1066 37 F3
The battle site, where Harold II defeated and killed his brother, Tostig, and Norwegian claimant to English throne, Harald Hardrada.

Battle of Towton 1461 36 C5
A battle site, where reputedly the largest and bloodiest battle ever fought on English soil took place. The Yorkists, led by Edward, Earl of March, defeated the Lancastrians, leaving 28,000 dead.

Beningbrough Hall 36 D3
The house was built by John Bourchier in 1716 (National Trust), with fine plasterwork and wood carving. It is set in a large park with gardens to the north west of Beningbrough. The Georgian Hall is hung with over 100 pictures from the National Portrait Gallery.

Bramham Park 36 C4
A 18c classical mansion surrounded by grounds modelled on those of Versailles, to the south west of Bramham.

Brimham Rocks 36 A2
A large group of rocks (National Trust) which have been fantastically shaped by erosion, to the east of Pateley Bridge.

Burnby Hall 37 G4
The two lakes display 80 varieties of hardy water lilies, which have been designated a National Collection. There is also a sporting trophy museum.

Byland Abbey 36 D1
The ruins of a 12c Cistercian monastery (English Heritage) located at the hamlet of Byland Abbey. The ruin of the church has a striking west front and notable patterned floor tiles.

Castle Howard 37 F1
A baroque 18c mansion by Vanbrugh surrounded by large formal grounds. It contains fine collections of furniture, paintings, ceramics and statuary.

☐ **Clifford's Tower** 5 E5
The remains of a 13c-14c stone tower (English Heritage) in a quatrefoil design, forming part of the York Castle fortifications. Built by Henry III to replace William the Conqueror's wooden keep which was razed in 1190, it sits atop a layered Norman motte, dominating York's skyline and affording fine views of the city.

Eden Camp 37 F1
A former prisoner of war camp, located to the north east of Malton, which recreates life in Britain during World War II by means of light, sound, smell and smoke.

☐ **Fairfax House** 5 E4
A museum of 18c life with a fine collection of period furniture and clocks in a Georgian town house in Castlegate.

Fountains Abbey 36 A2
The remains of this medieval Cistercian abbey (National Trust and English Heritage) beside the River Skell, are part of a World Heritage Site. The nearby, Fountains Hall, is a 17c house largely built with materials from the ruins of the abbey.

Gilling Castle 37 E1
The original 14c house has both Tudor and Georgian alterations, which is now a preparatory school for Ampleforth College. There are fine gardens in the grounds.

Golden Acre Park 36 A4
The 137 acres of gardens, lake and woodland to the south east of Bramhope were originally a large amusement park in the 1930s. The site is now a garden of botanical interest with rock, cottage and demonstration gardens. There is also a Display House for tender plants, old shrub roses, a pinetum and an arboretum. The park is notable for its spring and autumn colour.

Harewood House 36 B4
A mansion built in the 18c and 19c with landscaped grounds laid out by 'Capability' Brown. The formal Italian-style terrace was designed by Charles Barry in 1840.

Harlow Carr Botanical Gardens 36 A3
Headquarters of the Northern Horticultural Society set in 68 acres which are landscaped with woodland, herbaceous, rock, bog and alpine gardens. There also includes a Museum of Gardening and a model village.

Headingley 36 A5
Home to Yorkshire County Cricket Club and a Test match venue.

Impressions Gallery 5 E4
Located in a Georgian townhouse the gallery has contemporary photographic and new media exhibitions.

Isurium Roman Town 36 C2
A small Roman town (English Heritage) with a rectangular layout, on the north side of Aldborough. Some fragments of the town wall remain, and there are some interesting mosaics.

Jorvik Glass 37 F2
Demonstrations of glass-blowing and gift shop located in the grounds of Castle Howard.

Jorvik 5 E4
New JORVIK flies visitors through a dynamic, fresh vision of the City of York in the 10th Century. Technology of the 21st Century transforms real archaeological evidence, bringing New JORVIK, the trading hub of the Viking world dramatically to life.
24 hour Information Hotline 01904 643211.
JORVIK, Coppergate, York, YO1 9WT

Kirkham Priory 37 F2
Augustinian priory dating from the 12c (English Heritage), in the Derwent valley, south west of Malton. The late 13c gatehouse has magnificent heraldic shields.

Kirkstall Abbey 36 A5
The remains of 12c Cistercian church (English Heritage) by the River Aire, north west of Leeds. The gatehouse is now a museum.

Knaresborough Castle 36 B3
The ruined 14c castle of John of Gaunt, partly demolished by Roundheads. On the cliff top close to the market place in Knaresborough.

Lightwater Valley Park 36 A1
Located to the north west of Ripon. The attraction has rollercoaster rides, parkland, a farm and factory shopping outlets.

Lotherton Hall 36 C5
The former home of Lord and Lady Gascoigne, was completed at the beginning of the 20c. There is a museum of decorative arts containing the Gascoigne family's collection of paintings, jewellery, porcelain and silver. In the grounds there are formal Edwardian gardens. Wildlife on the estate includes two deer herds and a collection of over 200 bird species.

Markenfield Hall 36 A2
A turreted moated farmhouse dating from 14c. The original seat of the Markenfield family, which was forfeited by Sir Thomas Markenfield following his involvement in the 1569 rebellion against Queen Elizabeth I.

Merchant Adventurers' Hall 5 F4
The 14c Guildhall with a notable timbered Great Hall, in Fossgate.

Micklegate Bar Museum 4 C5
This 800-year-old royal gateway to York, in the city walls, houses a museum that portrays a civil and social insight into the history of York through scenic, graphic and tableaux format.

Mother Shipton's Cave **36 B3**
Located in Knaresborough Gorge, a legendary prophetess was reputed to have lived here in 15c, who predicted the invention of motor cars and aeroplanes. There is also a Petrifying Well, museum, playground and 12 acres of riverside grounds.

National Railway Museum **4 A2**
The railway heritage museum in York, is the largest in the world. There is a historic collection of locomotives and rolling stock including Mallard, the world's fastest steam locomotive, and Queen Victoria's personal saloon.

Newburgh Priory **36 D1**
There are remains of a monastery in the grounds of this 18c mansion.

Newby Hall **36 B2**
An 18c house, with interiors partly by Adam, which have recently been restored. The estate borders River Ure, to the west of Boroughbridge. The grounds contain the National Collection of Cornus plants.

Norton Conyers **36 B1**
Dating from medieval times with Stuart and Georgian additions, the house was visited by Charlotte Brontë and is linked to the novel, 'Jane Eyre'. The 18c walled garden has an orangery.

Nunnington Hall **37 E1**
This 17c manor and walled garden (National Trust) on the south side of the River Rye in the Vale of Pickering contains the Carlisle Collection of Miniature Rooms.

Old Malton Church **37 F1**
A 12c parish church, with a notable west front, north east of Malton. There are also relics of a Gilbertine priory founded circa 1150.

Ripley Castle **36 A2**
Located in Ripley Park, the castle was re-built in 1780, however the 15c gatehouse and 16c tower remain. The grounds were designed by 'Capability' Brown with the gardens containing the National Collection of Hyacinths, along with spring bulbs and tropical plants.

Ripon Cathedral **36 B1**
This 12c cathedral, with a Saxon crypt, is noted for the choir stalls and range of building styles from Saxon to Perpendicular.

Ripon Racecourse **36 B2**
Flat-racing course, with thirteen race days a year, which encircles a lake on the west side of the River Ure, to the south east of Ripon.

Roman Ridge **36 C5**
Roman road running from the Great North Road, east of Upton, through Castleford and Tadcaster, to York.

Royal Armouries Museum **36 B5**
Displays the history of armour and arms from 5BC to modern times, located in the centre of Leeds with five themed galleries; Orient, Hunting, Self-Defence, Tournament and War. There are demonstrations of jousting, falconery and poleaxe combat. Leatherworkers and gunmakers can be found in the Craft Centre and there is also a Menagerie.

Selby Abbey **37 E5**
An 11c limestone abbey with three towers.

Shandy Hall **36 D1**
A mid-15c house and garden on the west side of Coxwold. The house was the home of the 18c parson Lawrence Sterne, author of 'Tristram Shandy', between 1760 and 1768 and it contains the world's foremost collection of Sterne's novels. There is also a walled garden with old roses and a wild garden in an old quarry.

Spofforth Castle **36 B3**
The remains of a 14c fortified manor house owned by Percy family (English Heritage) west of Spofforth.

Steeton Hall **36 C5**
Remains of a medieval castle, situated west of South Milford. The gatehouse (English Heritage), probably dates from the 14c, and is well-preserved.

Stockeld Park **36 B4**
A small mansion designed by James Paine in Palladian style for the Middleton family, in the 18c and set in a large estate.

Studley Royal **36 A2**
The 18c water garden contains ornamental lakes, temples and statues. The estate includes the remains of the manor house which burnt down in 1945. St. Mary's Church (English Heritage), with it's highly decorated interior was designed in the 1870s by William Burges, but is no longer used for worship.

Sutton Park 36 D2
Early Georgian house, on the south side of Sutton-on-the-Forest. The house has magnificent plasterwork by Cortese and an important collection of porcelain and 18c furniture. The parkland was designed in a similar style to 'Capability' Brown, there are award winning gardens with a lily canal and woodland walks.

Temple Newsam 36 B5
A Tudor and Jacobean house and museum set in 1200 acres of parkland. The house contains a large collection of Chippendale furniture, a notable Picture Gallery and an 18c State Bed. The grounds include formal gardens, mixed woodland and Home Farm which is a rare breeds centre.

The Bar Convent 4 B5
Home of England's oldest active convent community, with museum illustrating York's early Christian history and life of the convent. Situated in Blossom Street, it contains a magnificent 18c domed chapel with priest's hiding hole.

The Minster (see p34) 5 E2
The largest medieval Gothic cathedral in Europe. The building was started in 1220, and took two-and-a-half centuries to complete. Noted for its stained glass, particularly the large east window, and rose window in south transept. The roof of the south transept was destroyed by fire in 1984; it was rebuilt using traditional methods.

Thicket Priory 37 E4
A Carmelite nunnery on the site of a 12c monastery, located to the south east of Wheldrake.

Treasurer's House 5 E1
Dating mainly from the 17c and 18c, although medieval in origin and once home of the Treasurers of York Minster. A fine collection of period furniture, china and glass.

Tropical World 36 B5
In Roundhay Park, north east of Leeds city centre, this attraction includes tropical plant houses which contain tropical fauna and flora, a butterfly house, a nocturnal house, and Coronation House with changing plant displays.

Wetherby Racecourse 36 C4
Located to the north east of Wetherby, adjacent to the A1 trunk road. National Hunt course, with fourteen race days a year.

Wharram Percy Village 37 G2
A deserted former medieval village (English Heritage) with only the church ruin remaining.

Wyville Animal Farm 37 F1
A working family farm with rare and older breeds, from cows to guinea pigs. Attractions include a farm shop, museum and local crafts.

York Castle Museum 5 F5
Located in York's old prison buildings in Tower Street, recording everyday life through the centuries and including a cobbled Victorian street full of shops, costume, social history, and military collections.

York City Art Gallery 4 D2
Paintings from the 15c to 20c including works by Bellotto, Reynolds, Lowry, Nash and York-born William Etty. Housed in a 19c Renaissance style building in Exhibition Square, York. There is also a collection of 20c studio pottery.

York Dungeon 5 E4
Museum of horrors in Clifford Street. Exhibits include the evocation of The Plague and encounters with Dick Turpin and Guy Fawkes.

York Racecourse 25 E2
Flat-racing course with fifteen race days each year, including the Ebor meeting in August.

Yorkshire Air Museum 37 E4
Over 30 historic aircraft, including a Halifax bomber, and aircraft equipment and memorabilia displayed at World War II bomber base, north east of Elvington. Airborne Forces Museum, Barnes Wallis Collection and a restored control tower with sound effects.

Yorkshire Museum 4 C2
Collections of Roman, Viking, Anglo-Saxon and medieval artefacts including the 15c Middleham Jewel, a gold pendant set with large sapphire; also decorative arts and natural history exhibits.

Yorkshire Museum of Farming 20 C2
An assortment of tools and machinery along with rare breeds of farm animals. There is also a reconstruction of James Herriot's surgery, blacksmith's shop, chapel, hardware shop and Land Army display. Other features include the Derwent Valley Light Railway, a Brigantium reconstruction of a Roman fort, a Danelaw reconstruction of a Dark Ages village, a gift shop, cafe and picnic/play area.

34 The Minster

The triple towers of the great Minster dominate York. The fifth church to stand upon the site, it is built on cruciform style and its chief characteristics, inside as outside, are great beauty and impressive size and space. The magnificent stained glass in the Minster - much of it medieval - is of tremendous interest. In the south transept the great Rose window displays a design entwining the red and white roses of Lancaster and York respectively, commemorating the wedding in 1486 of Henry VII to Elizabeth of York, which at last united the two warring 'Roses.' The Choir, the north transept and the octagonal Chapter House are very fine, the roof vaulting being among the best examples to be seen anywhere. Beyond the Close to the north of the Minster are the Deanery and the Library (Early English), the latter the depository of many literary treasures. The Minster itself is rich in historic possessions and is the seat of the second See of England, its Archbishop being next in rank and precedence to the Primate of All England, Archbishop of Canterbury. A fire in 1984 badly damaged the roof of the south transept but brave firefighting prevented it from spreading to the rest of the Cathedral.

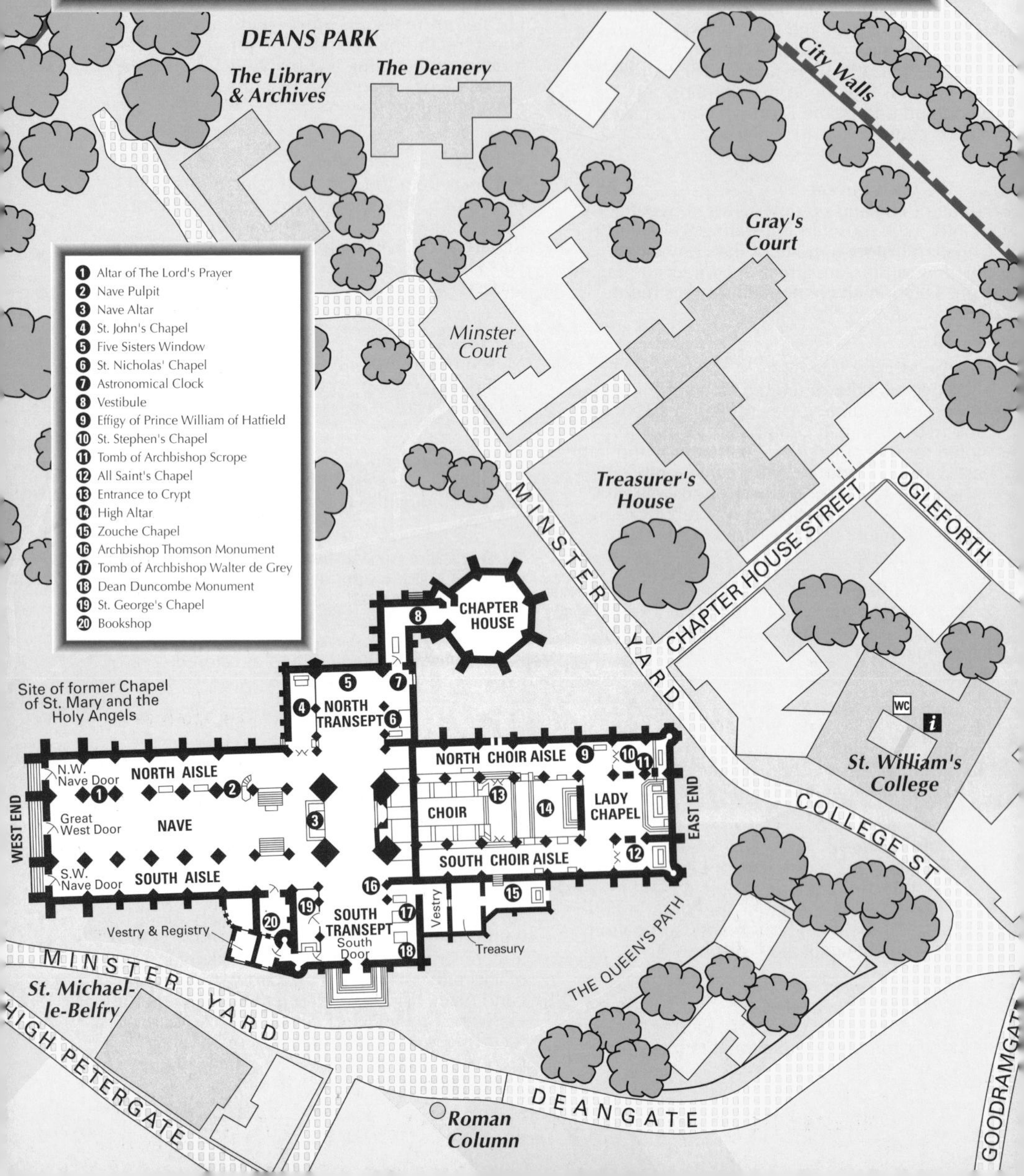

Key to Road Map Symbols

M1	Motorway
30 29	Motorway junctions (full, limited access)
	Motorway service areas (off road, full, limited access)
A19	Primary route (dual/single)
A163	'A' road (dual/single)
B1222	'B' road (dual/single)
	Minor road
	Restricted access due to road conditions or private ownership
	Road projected or under construction
	Multi-level junction
	Roundabout
10	Road distance in miles
	Road tunnel
	Steep hill (arrows point downhill)
Toll	Level crossing/Toll
	Railway line and station
	Railway tunnel
	Airport
	Canal / dry canal / canal tunnel
	Built up area
	Town / Village / Other settlement
Selby	Primary route destination
	County / Unitary Authority boundary
	National / Regional Park
	Forest Park boundary
430	National Grid reference
	Woodland
468	Spot height (metres)
491	Summit height (metres)
	Lake / Dam / River / Waterfall

More details of the places of interest shown on the mapping can be found on pages 30-33

	Tourist information office (all year / seasonal)
	Preserved railway
	Ancient monument
	Ecclesiastical building
	Historic house (with or without garden)
	Museum / Art gallery
	Factory shop village
1738	Battlefield
	Castle
	Garden
	Country park
	Nature reserve
	Theme park
	Racecourse
	Major sports venue
	Motor racing circuit
	Wildlife park or Zoo
	Other interesting feature
	Golf course
(NT)	National Trust property

	land below	0	165	490	985	1640	2295	2950	feet
water	sea level	0	50	150	300	500	700	900	metres

SCALE: 4 miles to 1 inch (10km to 4cm approx)

0 4 8 12 16 miles

0 5 10 15 20 25 kilometres

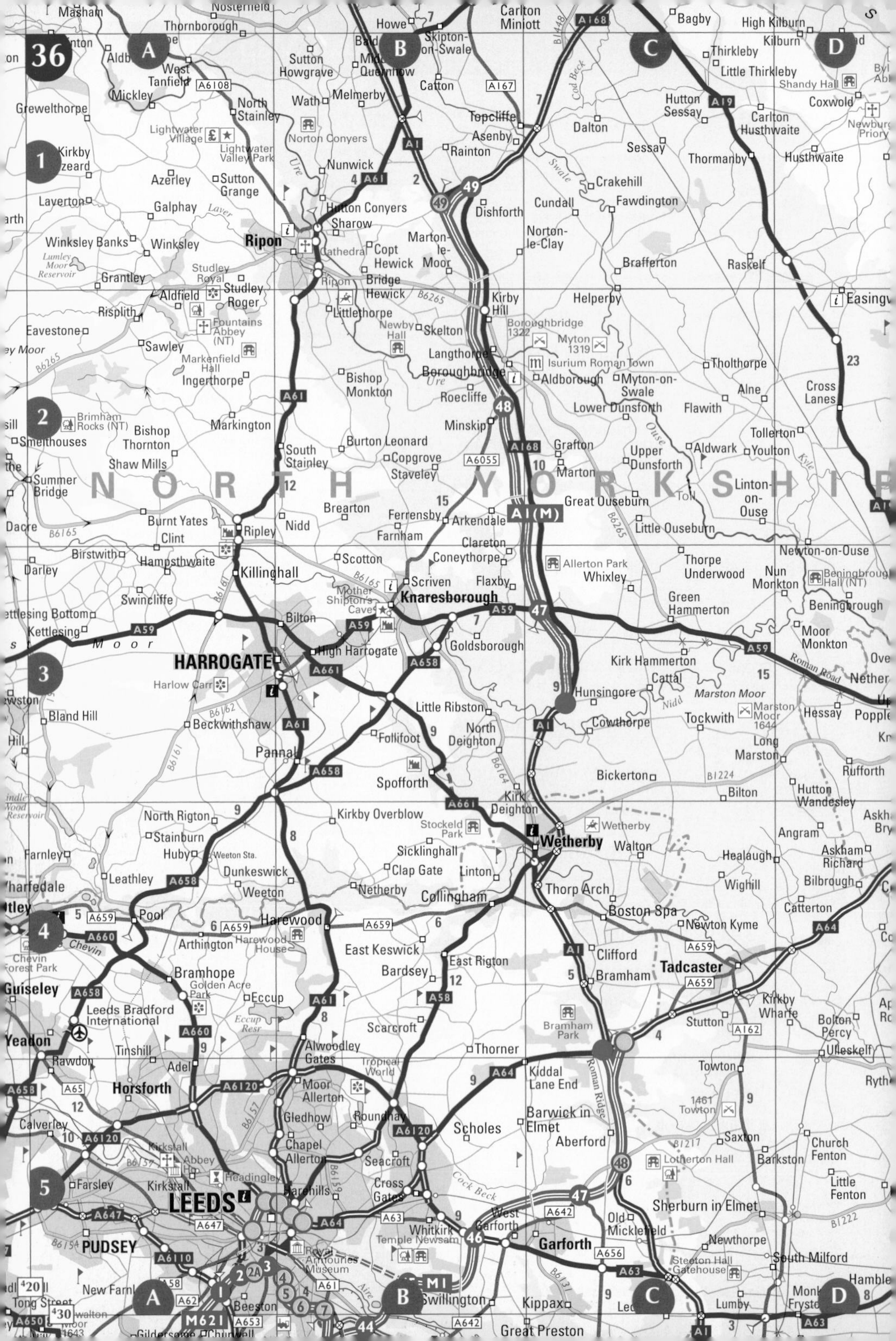
NORTH YORKSHIRE
Masham
Thornborough
West Tanfield
Mickley
Grewelthorpe
Kirkby Malzeard
Azerley
Laverton
Galphay
Winksley Banks
Winksley
Lumley Moor Reservoir
Grantley
Ripon
Cathedral
North Stainley
Lightwater Village
Lightwater Valley Park
Sutton Grange
Sutton Howgrave
Wath
Melmerby
Norton Conyers
Nunwick
Hutton Conyers
Sharow
Studley Royal
Studley Roger
Aldfield
Risplith
Fountains Abbey (NT)
Eavestone
Sawley
Markenfield Hall
Ingerthorpe
Brimham Rocks (NT)
Bishop Thornton
Markington
Smelthouses
Shaw Mills
Summer Bridge
Dacre
Burnt Yates
Clint
Ripley
Birstwith
Hampsthwaite
Darley
Killinghall
Swincliffe
Kettlesing Bottom
Kettlesing
HARROGATE
Harlow Carr
Bland Hill
Beckwithshaw
Pannal
Bilton
High Harrogate
Howe
Skipton-on-Swale
Middleton Quernhow
Catton
Carlton Miniott
Topcliffe
Asenby
Rainton
Dishforth
Marton-le-Moor
Copt Hewick
Bridge Hewick
Littlethorpe
Newby Hall
Skelton
Kirby Hill
Boroughbridge 1322
Myton 1319
Langthorpe
Boroughbridge
Isurium Roman Town
Aldborough
Bishop Monkton
Roecliffe
Minskip
South Stainley
Burton Leonard
Copgrove
Staveley
Brearton
Nidd
Ferrensby
Arkendale
Farnham
Scotton
Clareton
Coneythorpe
Allerton Park
Flaxby
Scriven
Mother Shipton's Cave
Knaresborough
Goldsborough
Bagby
High Kilburn
Kilburn
Thirkleby
Little Thirkleby
Shandy Hall
Hutton Sessay
Carlton Husthwaite
Coxwold
Newburgh Priory
Dalton
Sessay
Thormanby
Husthwaite
Crakehill
Cundall
Fawdington
Norton-le-Clay
Brafferton
Raskelf
Helperby
Easingwold
Tholthorpe
Myton-on-Swale
Alne
Cross Lanes
Lower Dunsforth
Flawith
Tollerton
Grafton
Upper Dunsforth
Aldwark
Youlton
Marton
Great Ouseburn
Little Ouseburn
Linton-on-Ouse
Thorpe Underwood
Whixley
Newton-on-Ouse
Nun Monkton
Beningbrough Hall (NT)
Beningbrough
Green Hammerton
Moor Monkton
Kirk Hammerton
Cattal
Marston Moor
Marston Moor 1644
Hunsingore
Cowthorpe
Tockwith
Hessay
Long Marston
Little Ribston
North Deighton
Follifoot
Spofforth
Kirk Deighton
Bickerton
Bilton
Rufforth
Hutton Wandesley
Wetherby
Walton
Angram
Askham Bryan
Askham Richard
Healaugh
Wighill
Bilbrough
Thorp Arch
Boston Spa
Newton Kyme
Catterton
Clifford
Bramham
Tadcaster
Bramham Park
Kirkby Wharfe
Stutton
Bolton Percy
Ulleskelf
Towton
1461 Towton
Saxton
Church Fenton
Barkston
Little Fenton
Lotherton Hall
Sherburn in Elmet
Old Micklefield
Newthorpe
South Milford
Steeton Hall Gatehouse
Hamble
Monk Fryston
Lumby
Ledsham
North Rigton
Stainburn
Huby
Weeton Sta.
Farnley
Leathley
Dunkeswick
Weeton
Wharfedale
Otley
Pool
Arthington
Harewood
Harewood House
Chevin Forest Park
Bramhope
Golden Acre Park
Eccup
Eccup Resr
Guiseley
Yeadon
Leeds Bradford International
Tinshill
Rawdon
Adel
Horsforth
Calverley
Kirkby Overblow
Stockeld Park
Sicklinghall
Clap Gate
Linton
Netherby
Collingham
East Keswick
Bardsey
East Rigton
Scarcroft
Thorner
Alwoodley Gates
Tropical World
Moor Allerton
Kiddal Lane End
Roman Ridge
Gledhow
Roundhay
Scholes
Barwick in Elmet
Aberford
Chapel Allerton
Seacroft
Kirkstall Abbey
Kirkstall
Headingley
Farsley
LEEDS
Harehills
Cross Gates
Whitkirk
West Garforth
Garforth
Temple Newsam
Royal Armouries Museum
PUDSEY
New Farnley
Tong Street
Beeston
Swillington
Kippax
Great Preston
Gildersome
Churwell
Adwalton Moor 1643
Cock Beck
Aire
Ure
Swale
Ouse
Nidd
Kyle
Laver
Cod Beck
Roman Road
Chevin
Moor
A1
A1(M)
A19
A61
A167
A168
A6108
A6055
A59
A658
A661
A659
A660
A6120
A65
A64
A58
A63
A642
A656
A162
A647
A6110
A62
A653
A650
M1
M621
B6265
B6165
B6161
B6162
B6164
B1224
B1217
B1222
B6157
B6159
B6154
B6131
B1448
A
B
C
D
1
2
3
4
5
20
30

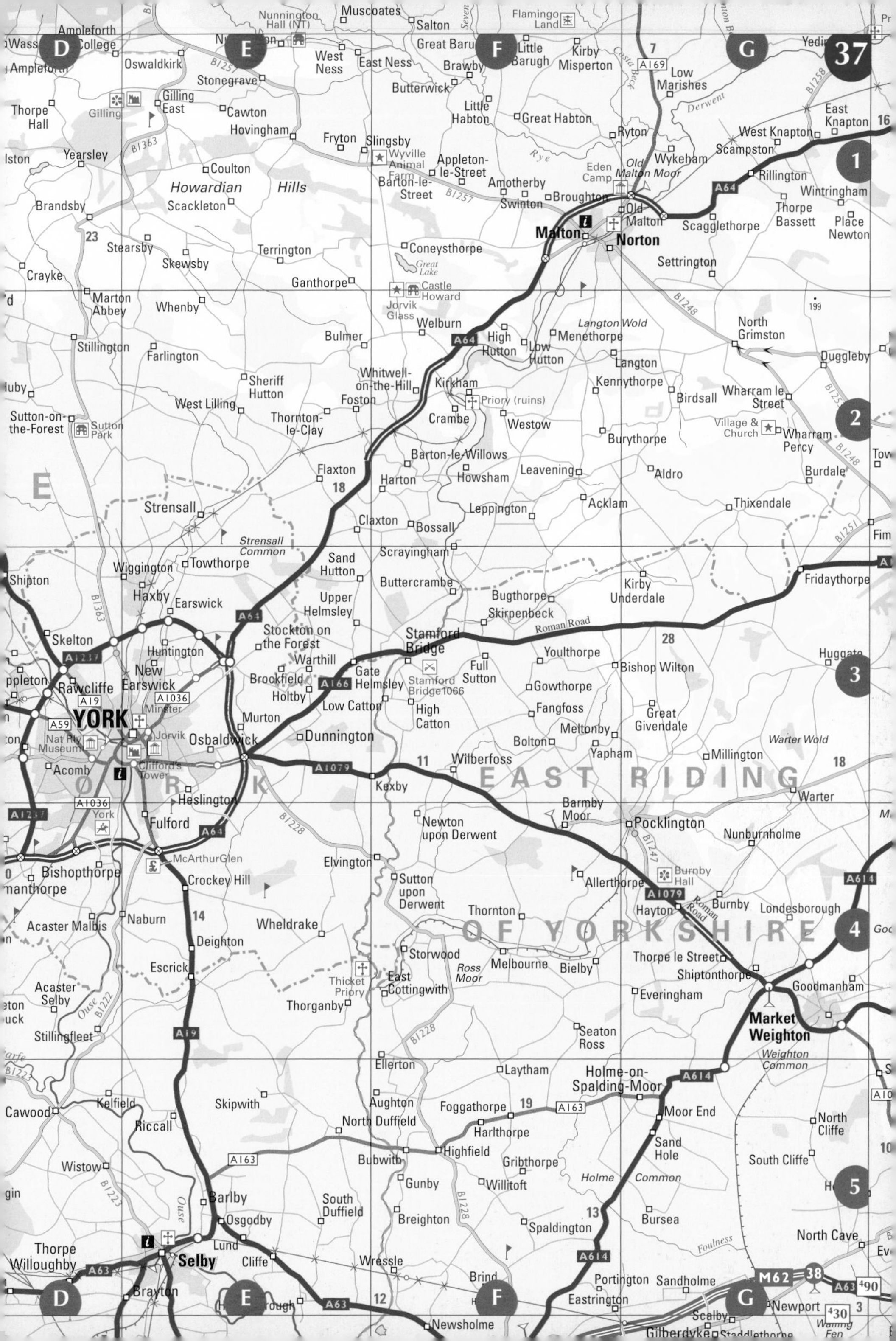
D
E
F
G
1
2
3
4
5
Ampleforth College
Wass
Ampleforth
Nunnington Hall (NT)
Muscoates
Salton
Seven
Flamingo Land
Oswaldkirk
West Ness
East Ness
Great Barugh
Little Barugh
Kirby Misperton
A169
Low Marishes
Yedingham
Stonegrave
B1257
Brawby
Butterwick
Costa Beck
Derwent
B1258
Thorpe Hall
Gilling
Gilling East
Cawton
Little Habton
Great Habton
Ryton
East Knapton
West Knapton
16
Hovingham
Fryton
Slingsby
Wyville Animal Farm
Appleton-le-Street
Barton-le-Street
Rye
Wykeham
Scampston
Eden Camp
Old Malton Moor
Rillington
B1363
Yearsley
Coulton
Howardian Hills
Amotherby
Swinton
Broughton
Old Malton
A64
Wintringham
Thorpe Bassett
Place Newton
Brandsby
Scackleton
B1257
Scagglethorpe
Malton
Norton
23
Stearsby
Terrington
Skewsby
Coneysthorpe
Great Lake
Settrington
Crayke
Ganthorpe
Castle Howard
Jorvik Glass
B1248
199
Marton Abbey
Whenby
Welburn
Langton Wold
North Grimston
Bulmer
High Hutton
Low Hutton
Menethorpe
Stillington
Farlington
Langton
Duggleby
Whitwell-on-the-Hill
Kirkham
Kennythorpe
Birdsall
Wharram le Street
Sheriff Hutton
Priory (ruins)
B1253
West Lilling
Foston
Crambe
Westow
Village & Church
Wharram Percy
Sutton-on-the-Forest
Sutton Park
Thornton-le-Clay
Burythorpe
B1248
Barton-le-Willows
Leavening
Aldro
Burdale
Flaxton
Harton
Howsham
18
Acklam
Thixendale
Strensall
Leppington
Claxton
Bossall
B1251
Strensall Common
Scrayingham
Sand Hutton
Wiggington
Towthorpe
Shipton
Buttercrambe
Kirby Underdale
Fridaythorpe
Haxby
Upper Helmsley
Bugthorpe
Earswick
Skirpenbeck
B1363
A64
Stockton on the Forest
Stamford Bridge
Roman Road
Skelton
Huntington
28
A1237
Warthill
Youlthorpe
Huggate
New Earswick
Full Sutton
Bishop Wilton
Rawcliffe
Brockfield
Gate Helmsley
Stamford Bridge 1066
A166
Gowthorpe
A19
A1036
Holtby
Minster
Low Catton
High Catton
Fangfoss
Great Givendale
A59
YORK
Jorvik
Murton
Nat Rly Museum
Osbaldwick
Dunnington
Meltonby
Bolton
Warter Wold
Yapham
Millington
Acomb
Clifford's Tower
A1079
11
Wilberfoss
18
Kexby
EAST RIDING
Warter
Heslington
A1036
York
B1228
Barmby Moor
Pocklington
Fulford
A64
Newton upon Derwent
Nunburnholme
B1247
McArthurGlen
Bishopthorpe
Elvington
Burnby Hall
Crockey Hill
Sutton upon Derwent
Allerthorpe
A1079
A614
Hayton
Roman Road
Burnby
Londesborough
Thornton
14
Acaster Malbis
Naburn
Wheldrake
OF YORKSHIRE
Deighton
Storwood
Thorpe le Street
Escrick
Ross Moor
Melbourne
Bielby
Shiptonthorpe
Thicket Priory
East Cottingwith
Goodmanham
Acaster Selby
Ouse
B1222
Thorganby
Everingham
Market Weighton
Stillingfleet
A19
Seaton Ross
B1228
Weighton Common
B1223
Ellerton
Laytham
Holme-on-Spalding-Moor
A614
Kelfield
Skipwith
Aughton
Foggathorpe
19
A163
Cawood
Moor End
North Cliffe
Riccall
North Duffield
Harlthorpe
Sand Hole
Highfield
A163
Bubwith
Gribthorpe
South Cliffe
Wistow
B1223
Holme
Common
Gunby
Willitoft
Ouse
Barlby
South Duffield
B1228
Osgodby
Breighton
Spaldington
13
Bursea
Thorpe Willoughby
Lund
Foulness
North Cave
Selby
Cliffe
Wressle
A614
A63
M62
38
A63
Brind
Portington
Sandholme
Brayton
Eastrington
A63
12
Newport
Newsholme
Gilberdyke
Scalby
Staddlethorpe
Walling Fen

Index to Street Names

General Abbreviations

All	Alley	Conv	Convent	Gdn	Garden	Ms	Mews	Sec	Secondary
Allot	Allotments	Cor	Corner	Gdns	Gardens	Mt	Mount	Shop	Shopping
Amb	Ambulance	Coron	Coroners	Govt	Government	Mus	Museum	Sq	Square
App	Approach	Cors	Corners	Gra	Grange	N	North	St.	Saint
Arc	Arcade	Cotts	Cottages	Grd	Ground	NT	National	St	Street
Ave	Avenue	Cov	Covered	Grds	Grounds		Trust	Sta	Station
Bdy	Broadway	Crem	Crematorium	Grn	Green	Nat	National	Sts	Streets
Bk	Bank	Cres	Crescent	Grns	Greens	PH	Public House	Sub	Subway
Bldgs	Buildings	Ct	Court	Gro	Grove	PO	Post Office	Swim	Swimming
Boul	Boulevard	Cts	Courts	Gros	Groves	Par	Parade	TA	Territorial
Bowl	Bowling	Ctyd	Courtyard	Gt	Great	Pas	Passage		Army
Br/Bri	Bridge	Dep	Depot	Ho	House	Pav	Pavilion	TH	Town Hall
C of E	Church of	Dev	Development	Hos	Houses	Pk	Park	Tenn	Tennis
	England	Dr	Drive	Hosp	Hospital	Pl	Place	Ter	Terrace
Cath	Cathedral	Dws	Dwellings	Hts	Heights	Pol	Police	Thea	Theatre
Cem	Cemetery	E	East	Ind	Industrial	Prec	Precinct	Trd	Trading
Cen	Central,	Ed	Education	Int	International	Prim	Primary	Twr	Tower
	Centre	Elec	Electricity	Junct	Junction	Prom	Promenade	Twrs	Towers
Cft	Croft	Embk	Embankment	La	Lane	Pt	Point	Uni	University
Cfts	Crofts	Est	Estate	Las	Lanes	Quad	Quadrant	Up	Upper
Ch	Church	Ex	Exchange	Lib	Library	RC	Roman	Vil	Villa, Villas
Chyd	Churchyard	Exhib	Exhibition	Lo	Lodge		Catholic	Vw	View
Cin	Cinema	FB	Footbridge	Lwr	Lower	Rd	Road	W	West
Circ	Circus	FC	Football Club	Mag	Magistrates	Rds	Roads	Wd	Wood
Cl	Close	Fld	Field	Mans	Mansions	Rec	Recreation	Wds	Woods
Co	County	Flds	Fields	Mem	Memorial	Res	Reservoir	Wf	Wharf
Coll	College	Fm	Farm	Mid	Middle	Ri	Rise	Wk	Walk
Comm	Community	Gall	Gallery	Mkt	Market	S	South	Wks	Works
Comn	Common	Gar	Garage	Mkts	Markets	Sch	School	Yd	Yard

District Abbreviations

A.Bry.	Askham Bryan	Hes.	Heslington	St.For.	Stockton on the Forest
A.Rich.	Askham Richard	Hunt.	Huntington	Stren.	Strensall
Bish.	Bishopthorpe	Midd.	Middlethorpe	Tow.	Towthorpe
Cop.	Copmanthorpe	N.Ears.	New Earswick	U.Pop.	Upper Poppleton
Drin.	Dringhouses	N.Pop.	Nether Poppleton	Wig.	Wigginton
Dun.	Dunnington	Osb.	Osbaldwick		
Ears.	Earswick	Skel.	Skelton		

There are entries in the index which are followed by a number in **bold**. These numbers can be found on the map where there is insufficient space to show the street name in full. For example the location of Abbot St **6** *YO31* 18 C1, will be found by a number 6 in the square C1 on page 18.

A

Abbey Ct *YO31*	13	F5
Abbey St *YO30*	17	H1
Abbot St **6** *YO31*	18	C1
Abbots Gait (Hunt.) *YO32*	8	C5
Abbotsford Rd *YO10*	19	E4
Abbotsway *YO31*	13	F5
Abelton Gro (Haxby) *YO32*	8	A3
Acacia Gro (Haxby) *YO32*	8	A2
Acaster La (Bish.) *YO23*	25	F5
Acomb Ms (Acomb) *YO24*	16	D4
Acomb Rd *YO24*	17	F4
Acomb Wd Cl *YO24*	24	A1
Acomb Wd Dr *YO24*	23	H2
Acorn Way *YO24*	24	B1
Adelaide St *YO23*	18	A6
Adlington Cl **3** (Stren.) *YO32*	9	F4
Agar St *YO31*	5	F1
Ainsty Ave *YO24*	24	D1
Ainsty Gro *YO24*	24	D1
Aintree Ct *YO24*	24	D1
Albany St **7** *YO26*	17	G2
Albemarle Rd *YO23*	17	H5
Albert Cl (Hunt.) *YO32*	13	F5
Albert St *YO10*	5	G5
Albion Ave *YO26*	16	C2
Albion St **9** *YO1*	4	D5
Alcelina Ct *YO23*	4	C6
Alcuin Ave *YO10*	19	F3
Aldborough Way *YO26*	17	G2
Alder Way (N.Ears.) *YO32*	13	E3
Alderley Ct (Hunt.) *YO32*	13	F2
Aldersyde *YO24*	24	C2
Aldreth Gro *YO23*	18	B6
Aldwark *YO1*	5	F2
Alexa Ct *YO24*	16	D4
Alexander Ave *YO31*	13	F3
Alexandra Ct *YO10*	18	D3
Alexandra Rd (Stren.) *YO32*	9	F6
Algarth Ri *YO31*	14	A6
Algarth Rd *YO31*	14	A6
All Saints La **11** *YO1*	4	D4
Allan St **2** *YO30*	12	D6
Allanson Gro **2** *YO24*	17	F5
Allen Cl *YO10*	19	F3
Allendale *YO24*	24	B1
Allerton Dr (N.Pop.) *YO26*	10	C3
Allington Dr *YO31*	19	G1
Alma Ct *YO10*	18	C5
Alma Gro *YO10*	18	C5
Alma Ter *YO10*	18	C5
Almery Ter *YO30*	4	B2
Almond Gro (N.Ears.) *YO32*	13	E1
Almsford Dr *YO26*	16	C2
Almsford Rd *YO26*	16	D2
Alne Ter *YO10*	18	D5
Alness Dr *YO24*	23	H2
Alvis Gro *YO10*	20	A3
Alwyne Dr *YO30*	11	H4
Alwyne Gro *YO30*	11	H4
Amber St **12** *YO31*	18	C1
Amberly St *YO26*	17	F2
Ambleside Ave *YO10*	19	G3
Ambrose St *YO10*	18	C6
Amy Johnson Way *YO30*	12	A2
Ancress Wk *YO23*	4	C6
Ancroft Cl **7** *YO1*	5	F5
Anderson Gro *YO24*	17	G5
Andrew Dr (Hunt.) *YO32*	13	G4
Angram Cl *YO30*	12	A4
Annan Cl *YO24*	24	A3
Anne St *YO23*	18	B5
Anson Dr *YO10*	25	H1
Anthea Dr *YO31*	13	F4
Apollo Ct **1** *YO10*	18	D5
Apollo St *YO10*	5	H6
Apple Garth (U.Pop.) *YO26*	10	C4
Appleby Glade (Haxby) *YO32*	8	A4
Appleby Pl *YO31*	19	F2
Applecroft Rd *YO31*	14	A6
Appleton Ct (Bish.) *YO23*	24	D6
Appleton Rd (Bish.) *YO23*	24	D6
Arbor Cl (Hunt.) *YO32*	13	F2
Arenhall Cl **1** (Wig.) *YO32*	7	H3
Argyle St *YO23*	18	A6
Arlington Rd *YO30*	12	B4
Arncliffe Ms *YO10*	18	C5
Arnside Pl *YO10*	19	E4
Arran Pl *YO31*	13	E6
Arthur Pl (Skel.) *YO30*	6	A6
Arthur St *YO10*	18	D4
Arundel Gro *YO24*	24	A2
Ascot Rd (Wig.) *YO32*	7	G1
Ascot Way *YO24*	17	E6
Ash Cl *YO31*	14	A6
Ash La (Haxby) *YO32*	8	A1
Ash St *YO26*	17	F3
Ash Wk (Stren.) *YO32*	9	G5

Ashbourne Way *YO24*	24	A1
Ashdale Rd (Dun.) *YO19*	21	H2
Ashfield Ct **2** *YO24*	24	C2
Ashford Pl *YO24*	17	E5
Ashley Pk Cres *YO31*	19	G1
Ashley Pk Rd *YO31*	14	A6
Ashmeade Cl *YO24*	23	H2
Ashton Ave *YO30*	12	C5
Ashville St *YO31*	13	E6
Ashwood Glade (Haxby) *YO32*	7	H5
Askham Bryan La (A.Bry.) *YO23*	23	F3
Askham Cft *YO24*	16	C6
Askham Flds La *YO23*	23	E4
Askham Gro *YO24*	16	C5
Askham La *YO24*	23	G1
Aspen Cl (Dun.) *YO19*	21	H1
Asquith Ave *YO31*	19	F2
Atcherley Cl *YO10*	25	G1
Atlas Rd *YO30*	12	B2
Aucuba Cl (N.Ears.) *YO32*	13	E3
Audax Rd *YO30*	12	B2
Auster Rd *YO30*	12	B2
Avenue, The *YO30*	17	H1
Avenue, The (Haxby) *YO32*	7	H1
Avenue, The (Park Estate) *YO32*	8	A3
Avenue Rd *YO30*	18	A1
Avenue Ter *YO30*	17	H1
Aviator Ct *YO30*	12	A3
Avon Dr (Hunt.) *YO32*	8	C5
Aylesham Ct (Hunt.) *YO32*	13	F2

B

Bachelor Hill *YO24*	16	D5
Back La (Cop.) *YO23*	22	A2
Back La (Knapton) *YO26*	16	B2
Back La (Wig.) *YO32*	7	G2
Back Swinegate **2** *YO1*	5	E3
Back W Vw **8** *YO30*	12	C6
Backhouse St **1** *YO31*	18	B1
Bad Bargain La *YO31*	19	F2
Badger Paddock **2** *YO31*	13	F3
Badger Wd Wk *YO10*	19	H5
Baildon Cl *YO26*	17	E3
Baile Hill Ter *YO1*	4	D6
Baker St *YO30*	12	C6
Balfour St *YO26*	17	G2
Balfour Way (Stren.) *YO32*	9	F5
Balmoral Ter *YO23*	18	A6
Bankside Cl (U.Pop.) *YO26*	10	C3
Bannisdale *YO24*	24	A2
Bar La *YO1*	4	B4
Barbara Gro *YO24*	17	G4
Barbers Dr (Cop.) *YO23*	22	B1
Barbican Ms *YO10*	5	H6
Barbican Pl *YO10*	5	G6
Barbican Rd *YO10*	5	G5
Barden Ct *YO30*	12	A4
Barfield Rd *YO31*	13	G5
Barker La *YO1*	4	C4
Barkston Ave *YO26*	16	B4
Barkston Cl *YO26*	16	B4
Barkston Gro *YO26*	16	B5
Barkston Rd *YO26*	16	B4
Barley Ri (Stren.) *YO32*	9	F5
Barley Vw (Haxby) *YO32*	7	H3
Barley Vw (Wig.) *YO32*	7	H3
Barleycorn Yd **10** *YO1*	5	F4
Barlow St *YO26*	17	E3
Barmby Ave *YO10*	26	A1
Barmby Cl **7** *YO30*	12	A4
Barnfield Way (Cop.) *YO23*	22	A3
Baron Glade *YO30*	11	H5
Barons Cres (Cop.) *YO23*	22	B2
Barrett Ave *YO24*	17	F4
Barstow Ave *YO10*	19	E4
Bartle Garth *YO1*	5	F2
Bateson Cl (Hes.) *YO10*	19	G6
Baysdale Ave *YO10*	20	A4
Beaconsfield St *YO24*	17	E4
Beadle Garth (Cop.) *YO23*	22	B2
Beagle Ridge Dr *YO24*	16	C6
Beans Way *YO31*	14	A5
Beaufort Cl *YO10*	19	G4
Beaulieu Cl (Hunt.) *YO32*	8	C6
Beaverdyke *YO30*	12	A4
Beck La *YO31*	19	F1
Beckfield La *YO26*	16	C3
Beckfield Pl *YO26*	16	C3
Beckwith Cl **1** *YO31*	14	B6
Bedale Ave *YO10*	20	A3
Bede Ave *YO30*	12	C6
Bedern *YO1*	5	F2
Beech Ave (Bish.) *YO23*	25	E6
Beech Ave *YO24*	17	G4
Beech Glade *YO31*	13	G3
Beech Gro (Acomb) *YO26*	16	D3
Beech Gro (U.Pop.) *YO26*	10	B4
Beech Pl (Stren.) *YO32*	9	F5
Beech Way (U.Pop.) *YO26*	10	C4
Beeches, The (Skel.) *YO30*	6	B6
Beechwood Glade *YO24*	16	C6
Beeforth Cl **3** (N.Ears.) *YO32*	13	E1
Belcombe Way **10** *YO30*	12	B6
Belgrave St *YO31*	12	D6
Bell Cl (Wig.) *YO32*	7	H3
Bell Fm Ave *YO31*	13	F5
Belle Vue St *YO10*	5	H6
Belle Vue Ter *YO10*	18	D4
Bellhouse Way *YO24*	23	H1
Bellmans Cft (Cop.) *YO23*	22	B2
Bellwood Dr *YO24*	23	H1
Belmont Cl *YO30*	12	A4
Beresford Ter *YO23*	18	B6
Berkeley Ter *YO26*	17	F2
Beverley Ct **2** *YO24*	17	E6
Beverley Gdns **3** *YO31*	18	D1
Bewlay St *YO23*	18	B5
Bilsdale Cl *YO30*	11	H3
Birch Cl **1** (N.Ears.) *YO32*	13	E3
Birch Copse **1** *YO24*	17	E5
Birch La (Haxby) *YO32*	8	A2
Birch Pk *YO31*	13	F4
Birch Tree Cl **4** (Stren.) *YO32*	9	F5
Birch Tree Ct **3** (Haxby) *YO32*	8	A2
Birkdale Gro *YO26*	16	C3
Birstwith Dr *YO26*	17	F3
Bishopgate St *YO23*	4	D6
Bishophill Junior *YO1*	4	C5
Bishophill Senior *YO1*	4	D5
Bishops Way *YO10*	19	H5
Bishopthorpe Rd *YO23*	25	G1
Bismarck St *YO26*	17	F2
Black Dikes La (U.Pop.) *YO26*	10	B5
Black Horse Pas **6** *YO1*	5	F4
Blacklee Cl (Stren.) *YO32*	9	H2
Blackthorn Dr *YO31*	13	F3
Blake St *YO1*	4	D2
Blakeley Gro **8** *YO30*	12	A2
Blakeney Pl *YO10*	18	D4
Bland La *YO26*	16	B3
Blatchford Ct **14** *YO30*	12	C5
Blatchford Ms **13** *YO30*	12	C5
Blenheim Ct **2** *YO30*	11	G2
Blossom St *YO24*	4	B6
Blue Br La *YO10*	18	C5
Board St **3** *YO23*	18	B5
Bog La *YO24*	23	H3
Bollans Ct **3** *YO1*	5	F2
Boltby Rd *YO30*	12	A3
Bonnington Ct **2** *YO26*	17	F3
Bootham *YO30*	4	C1
Bootham Bar *YO1*	4	D2
Bootham Cres *YO30*	18	A1
Bootham Row *YO30*	4	D1
Bootham Sq *YO30*	4	D1
Bootham Ter *YO30*	4	B1
Boothwood Rd **12** *YO30*	12	A3
Boroughbridge Rd *YO26*	11	E6
Borrowdale Dr *YO30*	12	A4
Bouthwaite Dr *YO26*	17	F3
Bowes Ave *YO31*	18	D2
Bowland Way *YO30*	12	B4
Bowling Grn Ct *YO31*	13	E5
Bowling Grn Cft *YO31*	13	E5
Bowling Grn La **9** *YO31*	18	C1
Bowness Dr *YO30*	11	H4
Bowyers Cl (Cop.) *YO23*	22	C1
Bracken Cl (Hunt.) *YO32*	13	G1
Bracken Hill *YO10*	19	H4
Bracken Rd *YO24*	24	D2
Brackenhills (U.Pop.) *YO26*	10	C4
Bradley Dr *YO24*	24	A1
Braeside Gdns *YO24*	17	F4
Brailsford Cres *YO30*	12	B5
Bramble Dene *YO24*	24	B2
Bramble Gro (Hunt.) *YO31*	13	F3
Bramham Ave *YO26*	16	B4
Bramham Gro *YO26*	16	B4
Bramham Rd *YO26*	16	B5
Bramley Garth *YO31*	19	G1
Brandon Gro *YO32*	14	D2
Brandsby Gro *YO31*	13	F3
Bransdale Cres *YO10*	20	A4
Bransholme Dr *YO30*	12	B3
Branton Pl *YO26*	16	B4
Bray Rd *YO10*	26	A1
Breary Cl *YO24*	17	G6
Brecks Cl **4** (Wig.) *YO32*	7	H3
Brecks La (Hunt.) *YO32*	13	G1
Brecksfield (Skel.) *YO30*	6	B6
Brentwood Cres *YO10*	19	H5
Bretgate **1** *YO1*	5	G5
Briar Ave *YO26*	16	C3
Briar Dr *YO31*	13	G4
Bridge Cl (Haxby) *YO32*	7	H4
Bridge La *YO31*	18	B1
Bridge Rd (Bish.) *YO23*	24	D6
Bridge St *YO1*	4	D4
Bridle Way **4** *YO26*	16	B4
Briergate (Haxby) *YO32*	8	A4
Briggs St *YO31*	12	D6
Bright St *YO26*	17	G2
Brinkworth Ter *YO10*	5	H5
Broad Acres (Haxby) *YO32*	7	H4
Broad Oak La **7** (Wig.) *YO32*	7	G2
Broadstone Way *YO30*	11	H2
Broadway *YO10*	25	H1
Broadway Gro *YO10*	26	A1
Broadway W *YO10*	25	H1
Brockfield Pk Dr *YO31*	13	F3
Brockfield Rd *YO31*	13	F3
Bromley St **8** *YO26*	17	G2
Brompton Rd *YO30*	12	B6
Brook St *YO31*	18	B1
Brooklands *YO10*	20	A3
Broome Cl (Hunt.) *YO32*	8	C6
Broome Rd **1** (Hunt.) *YO32*	8	D6
Broome Way (Hunt.) *YO32*	8	D6
Brougham Cl **3** *YO30*	12	A5
Broughton Way *YO10*	19	G3
Browney Cft *YO10*	5	F6
Brownlow St *YO31*	18	C1
Brunel Ct **9** *YO26*	17	G2
Brunswick St *YO23*	18	A6
Buckingham Ct **10** *YO1*	4	D5
Buckingham St *YO1*	4	D5
Bull La *YO10*	19	E4
Bull La (Heworth) *YO31*	19	E1
Burdyke Ave *YO30*	12	B5
Burgess Wk *YO24*	24	A1
Burlands La (U.Pop.) *YO26*	10	B6
Burlington Ave *YO10*	19	E3
Burnholme Ave *YO31*	19	F1
Burnholme Dr *YO31*	19	F1
Burnholme Gro *YO31*	19	F2
Burniston Gro *YO10*	19	F3
Burns Ct *YO24*	23	H2
Burnsall Dr *YO26*	17	F3
Burrill Ave *YO30*	12	C5
Burrill Dr (Wig.) *YO32*	7	F2
Burton Ave **7** *YO30*	12	C6
Burton Ct *YO30*	18	A1
Burton Stone La *YO30*	18	A1
Burtree Ave (Skel.) *YO30*	11	E1
Butcher Ter *YO23*	18	B6
Butt Hill **6** (Wig.) *YO32*	7	G2
Buttacre La (A.Rich.) *YO23*	22	B5
Butter Cl **4** (Wig.) *YO32*	7	G2
Buttermere Dr *YO30*	11	H4
Byland Ave *YO31*	13	F5
Byron Dr *YO30*	12	A5

C

Caedmon Cl *YO31*	13	H6

Cairnborrow *YO24*	23	H2
Caithness Cl **1** *YO30*	11	H2
Caldbeck Cl *YO30*	12	B4
Calder Ave (N.Pop.) *YO26*	11	E5
Calf Cl (Haxby) *YO32*	8	B3
Calvert Cl (Haxby) *YO32*	7	H4
Cambridge St *YO24*	4	A5
Cameron Gro *YO23*	18	B6
Campbell Ave *YO24*	17	F5
Campbell Ct *YO10*	19	G3
Campleshon Rd *YO23*	18	A6
Canham Gro *YO10*	20	A4
Canterbury Cl **9** (Wig.) *YO32*	7	G1
Carey St *YO10*	18	C6
Carl St **4** *YO23*	18	B5
Carleton St *YO26*	17	G2
Carlisle St *YO26*	17	G2
Carlton Ave *YO10*	19	G4
Carlton Cotts **11** (Wig.) *YO32*	7	G1
Carmelite St **5** *YO1*	5	F3
Carmires Ave (Haxby) *YO32*	8	B2
Carnot St *YO26*	17	G2
Carnoustie Cl *YO26*	16	C3
Caroline Cl *YO24*	17	G4
Caroline St **1** *YO23*	18	B5
Carr La *YO26*	17	E3
Carrfield *YO24*	24	A1
Carrick Gdns *YO24*	17	F4
Carrington Ave *YO26*	17	F2
Carrnock Ct *YO32*	13	G4
Carron Cres *YO24*	23	H2
Carrs La *YO1*	4	D5
Carter Ave *YO31*	19	E2
Castle Cl (Wig.) *YO32*	7	F1
Castle Mills Br *YO1*	5	F5
Castle Wk **14** *YO1*	5	E4
Castlegate *YO1*	5	E4
Cavendish Gro *YO10*	20	A4
Caxton Ave *YO26*	17	E1
Cayley Cl *YO30*	12	A4
Cecilia Pl **1** *YO24*	17	H4
Cedar Glade (Dun.) *YO19*	21	G2
Cedar Gro *YO31*	14	A6
Cedarwood Cl *YO24*	16	C6
Celtic Cl *YO26*	16	C2
Cemetery Rd *YO10*	18	C5
Centurion Pk *YO30*	12	C3
Chaldon Cl (Stren.) *YO32*	9	F5
Chalfonts *YO24*	17	G6
Chaloners Cres *YO24*	24	B2
Chaloners Rd *YO24*	24	B1
Chancery Ct (Acomb) *YO24*	16	D4
Chancery Ri *YO24*	17	G4
Chantry Ave (U.Pop.) *YO26*	10	C4
Chantry Cl *YO24*	24	A2
Chantry Gap (U.Pop.) *YO26*	10	C4
Chantry Gro (U.Pop.) *YO26*	10	C4
Chantry La (Bish.) *YO23*	25	F5
Chapel Flds Rd *YO26*	16	B4
Chapel La (A.Bry.) *YO23*	22	D4
Chapel Row **3** *YO1*	5	G5
Chapel Ter *YO24*	16	D4
Chapman's Ct *YO24*	24	B3
Chapter Ho St **4** *YO1*	5	E2
Charles Ct (Stren.) *YO32*	9	H3
Charles Moor *YO31*	13	G6
Charlotte St *YO10*	18	D3
Charlton St *YO23*	18	B5
Chaseside Ct *YO24*	24	C1
Chatsworth Ave (Stren.) *YO32*	9	H2
Chatsworth Dr (Haxby) *YO32*	8	C2
Chatsworth Ter *YO26*	17	F3
Chaucer La (Stren.) *YO32*	9	H2
Chaucer St **3** *YO10*	18	D4
Chaumont Way (St.For.) *YO32*	15	F1
Chelkar Way *YO30*	12	A4
Chelwood Wk *YO26*	17	F3
Cherry Garth *YO31*	19	G2
Cherry Gro **3** (U.Pop.) *YO26*	10	C4
Cherry Hill La **11** *YO23*	5	E6
Cherry La *YO24*	24	D1
Cherry Orchard **8** (Haxby) *YO32*	8	A3
Cherry Paddock (Haxby) *YO32*	8	A3
Cherry St *YO23*	18	B5
Cherry Tree Ave (N.Ears.) *YO32*	13	E1
Cherry Tree Ct **3** (Dun.) *YO19*	21	G2
Cherry Wd Cres (Fulford) *YO19*	26	A4
Chesney Flds *YO24*	17	E6
Chessingham Gdns *YO24*	24	C3
Chestnut Ave *YO31*	19	E1
Chestnut Ct (Hunt.) *YO32*	8	C6
Chestnut Gro *YO26*	16	D3
Chestnut Gro **4** (N.Ears.) *YO32*	13	F1
Chestnuts, The **2** (Wig.) *YO32*	7	H3
Cheviot Cl (Hunt.) *YO32*	13	G2
Chiltern Way (Hunt.) *YO32*	8	C6
Chipstead Wk **7** (Stren.) *YO32*	9	F4
Chudleigh Rd *YO26*	17	G2
Church Balk (Dun.) *YO19*	21	G1
Church Cl (A.Bry.) *YO23*	23	E3
Church La *YO1*	4	D4
Church La (Dun.) *YO19*	21	G1
Church La (Bish.) *YO23*	25	E5
Church La (N.Pop.) *YO26*	10	D3
Church La (Skel.) *YO30*	6	A6
Church La (Hunt.) *YO32*	8	C6
Church La (Stren.) *YO32*	9	F3
Church La (Wig.) *YO32*	7	H2
Church Ms **2** (Acomb) *YO26*	16	D4
Church Rd *YO10*	19	H3
Church St *YO1*	5	E3
Church St (Dun.) *YO19*	21	G1
Church St (Cop.) *YO23*	22	A2
Church Vw (Skel.) *YO30*	6	A5
Churchfield Dr (Wig.) *YO32*	7	H2
Cinder La *YO26*	4	A2
Cinder La *YO31*	18	D1
Cinder Ms *YO26*	17	H2
Clarence St *YO31*	18	B1
Clarendon Ct *YO31*	12	D6
Clarendon St **5** *YO31*	12	D6
Clarks Ter **1** (Heworth) *YO31*	19	E1
Clay Pl *YO24*	16	D6
Claygate *YO31*	19	G1
Clement St **4** *YO23*	4	D6
Clementhorpe *YO23*	4	D6
Cleveland St *YO24*	17	G3
Cleveland Ter **3** (Hunt.) *YO32*	13	G1
Cleveland Way (Hunt.) *YO32*	13	G2
Clifford St *YO1*	5	E4
Clifton *YO30*	12	B6
Clifton Br *YO26*	17	G1
Clifton Br *YO30*	17	G1
Clifton Dale *YO30*	17	H1
Clifton Grn *YO30*	17	H1
Clifton Moor Gate *YO30*	12	A2
Clifton Moor Retail Pk *YO30*	12	B1
Clifton Pl *YO30*	12	B6
Clive Gro *YO24*	17	G5
Cloisters Wk *YO31*	5	F2
Cloither Ct (Cop.) *YO23*	22	C1
Close, The *YO30*	12	A5
Coda Ave (Bish.) *YO23*	25	F6
Coeside *YO24*	23	H2
Coffee Yd *YO1*	5	E3
Coggan Cl *YO23*	18	A5
Coggan Way (Bish.) *YO23*	24	D5
Cole St **3** *YO31*	18	B1
Coledale Cl *YO30*	12	A4
Colenso St **5** *YO23*	5	E6
College Rd (Cop.) *YO23*	22	A1
College St *YO1*	5	E2
Colliergate *YO1*	5	E3
Collingham Pl **2** *YO26*	16	C3
Collingwood Ave *YO24*	17	G5
Common Rd (Dun.) *YO19*	21	H1
Compton St *YO30*	17	H1
Concorde Way *YO30*	12	B2
Coney St *YO1*	4	D3
Coneycroft (Dun.) *YO19*	21	H1
Conifer Cl **5** (N.Ears.) *YO32*	13	E3
Coniston Cl *YO30*	11	H4
Coniston Dr *YO10*	19	G3
Connaught Ct *YO10*	25	H1
Connaught Way (Hunt.) *YO32*	8	C5
Constantine Ave *YO10*	19	E3
Conway Cl **2** *YO30*	11	H2
Coopers Dr (Cop.) *YO23*	22	B1
Coopers Yd *YO1*	5	F4
Copmanthorpe La *YO23*	24	D6
Copper Beech Cl (Dun.) *YO19*	21	G1
Copper Beech Cl (U.Pop.) *YO26*	10	B5
Copper Beeches, The (Dun.) *YO19*	21	G1
Coppergate *YO1*	5	E4
Coppergate Wk *YO1*	5	E4
Coppice, The (Bish.) *YO23*	24	D5
Coppice Cl (Haxby) *YO32*	8	A1
Copwood Gro **5** (Wig.) *YO32*	7	H3
Corban La (Wig.) *YO32*	6	D1
Corban Way **5** (Wig.) *YO32*	7	G2
Corlett Ct *YO24*	24	A1
Cornborough Ave *YO31*	19	E2
Corncroft (Stren.) *YO32*	9	F5
Corner Cl (Wig.) *YO32*	7	F2
Cornlands Rd *YO24*	16	C6
Cornwall Dr *YO10*	26	A1
Cornwood Way (Haxby) *YO32*	7	H3
Cosmo Ave *YO31*	19	E2
Cotswold Way (Hunt.) *YO32*	8	D6
Cottage Ms **1** *YO31*	19	F1
Count de Burgh Ter *YO23*	18	A6
Courcey Gro *YO26*	16	D3
Courtyard, The (Bish.) *YO23*	25	E5
Covert, The *YO24*	24	D2
Coxlea Gro *YO31*	19	G1
Crab Tree Gro (N.Ears.) *YO32*	13	E2
Cranbrook Ave *YO26*	16	D2
Cranbrook Rd *YO26*	16	D1
Cranefield Pl *YO24*	24	A1
Crawley Way **2** *YO31*	19	G1
Creaser Cl (Stren.) *YO32*	9	F4
Crescent, The (Hes.) *YO10*	19	H6
Crescent, The *YO24*	4	B5
Crescent Rd *YO19*	26	B4
Crichton Ave *YO30*	12	C5
Crinan Ct (Hunt.) *YO32*	8	C5
Croft, The **1** (Stren.) *YO32*	9	G5
Croft Ct (Bish.) *YO23*	25	E5
Croft Fm Cl (Cop.) *YO23*	22	B1
Croft Side **3** *YO26*	16	C4
Croft Way *YO26*	16	C4
Crombie Ave *YO30*	12	C6
Cromer St *YO30*	12	C6
Cromwell Rd *YO1*	4	D5
Crooklands La (Haxby) *YO32*	8	A1
Cross La (Fulford) *YO19*	26	B4
Cross St **4** *YO24*	16	D4
Crossfield Cres (Fulford) *YO19*	26	A3
Crosslands Rd *YO10*	26	A1
Crossway, The *YO31*	13	F5
Crossways *YO10*	19	H5
Crummock *YO24*	24	A2
Cumberland Cl **4** (Stren.) *YO32*	9	G5
Cumberland St *YO1*	5	E4
Cumbrian Ave (Stren.) *YO32*	9	G5
Curlew Glebe (Dun.) *YO19*	21	G2
Curzon Ter *YO23*	18	A6
Custance Wk *YO23*	4	C6
Cycle St **4** *YO10*	19	F4
Cygnet St *YO23*	4	C6
Cyprus Gro (Haxby) *YO32*	7	H1

D

Dalby Mead *YO31*	13	G4
Dale Dyke Gro *YO30*	12	A3
Dale St *YO23*	4	C6
Dales La *YO31*	19	E1
Dalguise Gro *YO31*	18	C1
Dalmally Cl *YO24*	23	H3
Dalton Ter *YO24*	4	A6
Damson Cl **5** *YO26*	17	F3
Dane Ave *YO26*	16	D3
Danebury Ct *YO26*	16	D3
Danebury Cres *YO26*	16	D3
Danebury Dr *YO26*	16	D4
Danes Cft *YO10*	25	H1
Danesfort Ave *YO24*	16	D5
Danesgate **1** *YO26*	16	D3
Danesmead Cl *YO10*	25	H1
Danum Dr *YO10*	26	A1
Danum Rd *YO10*	25	H1
Darbie Cl **5** (N.Ears.) *YO32*	13	E1
Darfield Cl (Stren.) *YO32*	9	H2

Darnborough St *YO23* 4 D6
Darnbrook Wk *YO31* 19 F2
Davygate *YO1* 4 D3
Daysfoot Ct *YO10* 18 D4
De Grey Ct *YO30* 18 A1
De Grey Pl (Bish.) *YO23* 25 F6
De Grey St *YO31* 5 E1
De Grey Ter *YO31* 18 B1
De Mauley Pl (St.For.) *YO32* 15 F1
De Mowbray Ct (A.Rich.) *YO23* 22 A4
Deacons Ct (Cop.) *YO23* 22 B2
Dealtry Ave (Wig.) *YO32* 7 H3
Deangate *YO1* 5 E2
Deanhead Gro **1** *YO30* 11 H3
Deans Cl *YO23* 24 D5
Deans Pk *YO1* 5 E1
Dee Cl *YO24* 23 H2
Deepdale *YO24* 24 B1
Deer Hill Gro *YO30* 12 A2
Deerstone Way (Dun.) *YO19* 21 H2
Del Pyke **5** *YO31* 18 B1
Delamere Cl (Wig.) *YO32* 7 G1
Dell, The (Skel.) *YO30* 6 A6
Delwood (Fulford) *YO10* 25 H2
Dennis St *YO1* 5 F4
Dennison St *YO31* 18 C1
Deramore Dr *YO10* 19 H4
Deramore Dr W *YO10* 19 H5
Derwent Ave *YO10* 19 E3
Derwent Bungalows **1** (Dun.) *YO19* 21 F2
Derwent Ct **2** (Dun.) *YO19* 21 F2
Derwent Est (Dun.) *YO19* 21 F2
Derwent La (Dun.) *YO19* 21 G2
Derwent Rd *YO10* 25 H1
Derwent Wk (Hunt.) *YO32* 8 C6
Deveron Way *YO24* 23 H2
Devon Pl *YO10* 19 E4
Dewsbury Cotts **1** *YO1* 4 C5
Dewsbury Ter *YO1* 4 C5
Diamond St *YO31* 18 C1
Dickens Cl (Hunt.) *YO32* 13 F5
Dijon Ave *YO24* 16 D5
Dike Ray Cl (Haxby) *YO32* 7 H4
Dikelands Cl (U.Pop.) *YO26* 10 C4
Dikelands La (U.Pop.) *YO26* 10 C3
Dilys Gro *YO26* 17 F3
Disraeli Cl (Hunt.) *YO32* 13 F4
Dixon La *YO1* 5 F5
Dixons Yd *YO1* 5 F4
Dodgson Ter *YO26* 17 E3
Dodsworth Ave *YO31* 13 F6
Doe Pk *YO30* 12 A3
Doherty Wk *YO24* 24 A1
Don Ave *YO24* 24 C1
Doriam Ave *YO31* 13 G3
Doriam Dr *YO31* 13 F3
Dove St *YO23* 4 C6
Dower Ct *YO10* 18 D5
Drake St **2** *YO23* 4 D6
Drakes Cl (Hunt.) *YO32* 8 C6
Drapers Cft (Cop.) *YO23* 22 B1
Driffield Ter *YO24* 17 H5
Dringfield Cl *YO24* 24 B1
Dringthorpe Rd *YO24* 24 D2
Drome Rd (Cop.) *YO23* 22 C2
Drummond Vw (Bish.) *YO23* 25 F5
Dudley Ms **11** *YO31* 18 C1
Dudley St **10** *YO31* 18 C1
Duncombe Dr (Stren.) *YO32* 9 H2
Duncombe Pl *YO1* 4 D2
Dundas St *YO1* 5 F3
Durlston Dr (Stren.) *YO32* 9 F5
Dykes La (Cop.) *YO23* 22 A3

E

Eades Cl *YO30* 11 H5
Earle St *YO31* 18 C1
Earlsborough Ter *YO30* 4 B2
Earswick Chase (Ears.) *YO32* 8 C4
Earswick Village (Ears.) *YO32* 8 C4
Eason Rd *YO24* 24 C1
Eason Vw *YO24* 24 B1
East Cotts *YO30* 12 A5
East Mt Rd *YO24* 4 B6
East Par *YO31* 18 D2
East Way *YO31* 13 F3
Eastbourne Gro *YO31* 19 E2
Eastern Ter *YO31* 18 D1
Eastfield Ave (Haxby) *YO32* 7 H4
Eastfield Ct *YO10* 19 H5
Eastfield Cres *YO10* 19 H5
Eastfield La (Dun.) *YO19* 21 G1
Eastholme Dr *YO30* 11 H4
Easthorpe Dr (N.Pop.) *YO26* 10 D4
Eastland Ave **1** *YO24* 17 F5
Eastmoor Gdns (Fulford) *YO19* 26 B4
Eastward Ave *YO10* 26 A2
Eaton Ct *YO24* 23 H1
Ebor Cl (U.Pop.) *YO26* 10 C4
Ebor St *YO23* 18 B5
Ebor Way (N.Pop.) *YO26* 10 C3
Ebor Way (U.Pop.) *YO26* 10 C3
Ebsay Dr *YO30* 12 A3
Eden Cl *YO24* 24 A2
Edgware Rd *YO10* 18 C5
Eighth Ave *YO31* 19 E2
Elands Yd **2** *YO1* 5 G5
Elder Gro (Haxby) *YO32* 7 H2
Eldon St *YO31* 18 C1
Eldon Ter *YO31* 18 C1
Eldwick Cl *YO30* 12 A4
Eliot Ct (Fulford) *YO10* 25 H2
Ellwood Ct *YO10* 18 C5
Elm Gro *YO31* 13 G3
Elm Tree Ave (U.Pop.) *YO26* 10 C3
Elm Tree Gdns **3** *YO24* 16 D4
Elma Gro *YO30* 11 H3
Elmfield Ave *YO31* 13 G5
Elmfield Ter *YO31* 13 G6
Elmlands Gro *YO31* 13 G6
Elmpark Vale *YO31* 13 H6
Elmpark Vw *YO31* 13 H5
Elmpark Way *YO31* 13 H5
Elston Cl *YO30* 12 B5
Elvington La (Dun.) *YO19* 20 D3
Elvington La (Grimston) *YO19* 21 E5
Elvington Ter *YO10* 5 H4
Elwick Gro **3** *YO10* 19 H3
Embleton Dr *YO30* 12 A4
Emerald St *YO31* 18 C1
Emmerson St **2** *YO31* 18 D2
Endfields Rd *YO10* 26 A1
Enfield Cres *YO24* 17 G4
Ennerdale Ave *YO31* 19 G2
Escrick St *YO10* 5 F6
Esk Dr (N.Pop.) *YO26* 11 E5
Eskdale Ave *YO10* 19 H4
Esplanade, The *YO30* 4 A1
Esplanade Ct *YO30* 4 B2
Etive Pl *YO24* 23 H2
Eton Dr (Wig.) *YO32* 7 G1
Etty Ave *YO10* 19 F3
Eva Ave *YO30* 11 G3
Evelyn Cres *YO30* 12 C6
Exhibition Sq *YO1* 4 D2
Exhibition Sq *YO30* 4 D2

F

Faber Cl (Cop.) *YO23* 22 B1
Faber St *YO31* 5 H2
Fairfax Cft (Cop.) *YO23* 22 B2
Fairfax St *YO1* 4 C5
Fairfields Dr (Skel.) *YO30* 6 A6
Fairway *YO30* 12 B5
Fairway Dr (U.Pop.) *YO26* 10 C4
Falcon Cl (Haxby) *YO32* 8 B2
Falconer St *YO24* 17 G4
Falkland St **7** *YO1* 4 D5
Falsgrave Cres *YO30* 12 C6
Farfield *YO26* 16 D1
Farmers Way (Cop.) *YO23* 22 B1
Farmlands Rd *YO24* 24 B1
Farmstead Ri (Haxby) *YO32* 8 A4
Farndale Ave *YO10* 19 H3
Farndale St *YO10* 18 C5
Farrar St *YO10* 18 D4
Farriers Cft **2** (Cop.) *YO23* 22 B1
Fawcett St *YO10* 5 F6
Fawkes Dr *YO26* 16 D3
Feasegate **9** *YO1* 5 E3
Fellbrook Ave *YO26* 16 C3
Fenwick St *YO23* 18 B5
Fenwicks La (Fulford) *YO10* 25 H2
Ferguson Way (Hunt.) *YO32* 13 G4
Fern Cl (Hunt.) *YO32* 13 G1
Fern St *YO31* 5 F1
Fernway *YO10* 19 H4
Ferry La (Bish.) *YO23* 25 F5
Ferrymans Wk **1** (N.Pop.) *YO26* 10 C3
Fetter La *YO1* 4 D4
Feversham Cres *YO31* 12 D6
Fewster Way *YO10* 5 F6
Fewston Dr *YO30* 12 A4
Field La *YO10* 19 G5
Field Vw *YO30* 12 D6
Fifth Ave *YO31* 5 H1
Filey Ter *YO30* 12 D6
Finkle St *YO1* 5 E3
Finsbury Ave *YO23* 18 B6
Finsbury St *YO23* 18 B6
Fir Heath Cl *YO24* 16 D6
Fir Tree Cl (Ears.) *YO32* 8 C4
Firbank Cl **4** (Stren.) *YO32* 9 F4
First Ave *YO31* 19 E1
Firtree Cl *YO24* 17 F4
Firwood Whin **1** *YO31* 13 G3
Fishergate *YO10* 5 F5
Fishergate Bar *YO1* 5 G5
Fitzroy Ter *YO10* 5 G6
Flavian Gro *YO30* 12 A5
Flaxman Ave *YO10* 19 F3
Flaxman Cft (Cop.) *YO23* 22 B1
Flaxton Rd (Stren.) *YO32* 9 H4
Fleming Ave *YO31* 18 D2
Fletcher Ct **1** (Wig.) *YO32* 7 H2
Fletchers Cft **1** (Cop.) *YO23* 22 C1
Florence Gro *YO30* 11 G3
Fold Wk (Stren.) *YO32* 9 H2
Folks Cl (Haxby) *YO32* 8 B2
Fordlands Cres (Fulford) *YO19* 26 A3
Fordlands Rd (Fulford) *YO19* 26 B5
Forest Cl (Wig.) *YO32* 7 G3
Forest Ct **2** (Stren.) *YO32* 9 F4
Forest Gro *YO31* 19 E1
Forest Way *YO31* 19 E1
Foresters Wk *YO24* 16 C6
Forestgate (Haxby) *YO32* 7 H4
Forge Cl (Hunt.) *YO32* 13 G3
Forth St *YO26* 17 G1
Foss Br *YO1* 5 F4
Foss Ct *YO31* 13 F4
Foss Islands Rd *YO31* 5 G3
Foss Wk (N.Pop.) *YO26* 11 E5
Fossbank *YO31* 5 G2
Fossgate *YO1* 5 F4
Fossland Vw (Stren.) *YO32* 9 F4
Fossway *YO31* 13 F6
Foston Gro *YO31* 13 G5
Foundry La *YO26* 17 G2
Fountayne St *YO31* 12 D6
Fourth Ave *YO31* 18 D2
Fox Covert *YO31* 13 G3
Fox Garth (N.Pop.) *YO26* 10 D2
Foxcroft (Haxby) *YO32* 7 H5
Foxthorn Paddock *YO10* 20 A4
Foxton *YO24* 24 A1
Foxwood La *YO24* 23 H1
Frances St *YO10* 18 C6
Frederic St *YO30* 4 B2
Freemans Ct **2** *YO30* 12 B6
Friargate **16** *YO1* 5 E4
Friars Ter **12** *YO1* 5 E5
Friars Wk *YO31* 13 F6
Front St (Acomb) *YO24* 16 D4
Fryers Ct (Murton) *YO19* 20 D2
Fulford Ct *YO19* 25 H4
Fulford Cross *YO10* 18 C6
Fulford Ind Est *YO10* 18 C6
Fulford Ms (Fulford) *YO10* 26 A3
Fulford Pk (Fulford) *YO10* 25 H2
Fulford Rd *YO10* 18 C6
Fulfordgate *YO10* 26 A2

Furness Dr *YO30* 11 H4
Furnwood (Haxby) *YO32* 7 H4
Fylingdales Ave *YO30* 11 H5

G

Gainsborough Cl (Stren.) *YO32* 9 H2
Gale Fm Ct *YO24* 16 D4
Gale La *YO24* 16 D4
Galligap La *YO10* 19 H2
Gallops, The *YO24* 23 H1
Galmanhoe La *YO30* 4 C1
Galtres Ave *YO31* 14 A6
Galtres Gro *YO30* 12 A6
Galtres Rd *YO31* 14 A5
Ganton Pl *YO24* 24 C2
Garbett Way (Bish.) *YO23* 25 F6
Garburn Gro *YO30* 11 H4
Garbutt Gro *YO26* 17 E2
Garden Flats La (Dun.) *YO19* 21 G1
Garden Pl *YO1* 5 F3
Garden St *YO31* 18 B1
Gardeners Cl (Cop.) *YO23* 22 B1
Garfield Ter *YO26* 17 G2
Garland St **8** *YO26* 17 F3
Garlands, The *YO30* 12 B5
Garnet Ter *YO26* 17 F2
Garrow Hill *YO10* 19 E4
Garrow Hill Ave *YO10* 19 F4
Garrowby Way (Hes.) *YO10* 26 D1
Garth Ct (Hunt.) *YO32* 13 H1
Garth Rd (Hunt.) *YO32* 13 G1
Garth Ter *YO30* 12 C6
Garth Way (N.Ears.) *YO32* 13 E2
Garths End *YO10* 26 A1
Garths End (Haxby) *YO32* 8 C2
Gascoigne Wk *YO23* 4 D6
Gateland Cl (Haxby) *YO32* 7 H4
Gay Meadows (St.For.) *YO32* 15 G1
Geldof Rd (Hunt.) *YO32* 13 G4
George Cayley Dr *YO30* 12 B2
George Ct *YO31* 5 F1
George Hudson St *YO1* 4 C4
George St *YO1* 5 F5
Gerard Ave *YO31* 19 F2
Giles Ave *YO31* 19 F2
Gillamoor Ave **3** *YO31* 19 G2
Gillingwood Rd *YO30* 12 A2
Gillygate *YO31* 4 D1
Girvan Cl *YO24* 23 H2
Givendale Gro **6** *YO10* 19 H4
Glade, The *YO31* 14 A6
Gladstone St (Acomb) *YO24* 17 E4
Gladstone St *YO31* 18 C1
Glaisby Ct *YO31* 19 F1
Glaisdale *YO24* 24 B2
Glebe, The (Dun.) *YO19* 21 G1
Glebe Ave *YO26* 17 E2
Glebe Cl (Stren.) *YO32* 9 G4
Glebe Way (Haxby) *YO32* 7 H2
Glen Ave *YO31* 5 H1
Glen Cl (Fulford) *YO10* 26 A3
Glen Rd *YO31* 18 D2
Glencoe St **9** *YO30* 12 C6
Glenridding *YO24* 24 B2
Goodramgate *YO1* 5 E3
Goodwood Gro *YO24* 17 G6
Gordon St *YO10* 5 H6
Gormire Ave *YO31* 13 F3
Gorse Hill (Dun.) *YO19* 21 H1
Gorse Paddock *YO31* 13 G3
Gouthwaite Cl *YO30* 12 A3
Government Ho Rd *YO30* 17 G1
Gower Rd *YO24* 24 C1
Grampian Cl (Hunt.) *YO32* 8 C6
Granary Ct **22** *YO1* 5 E3
Grange Cl (Skel.) *YO30* 6 A6
Grange Garth *YO10* 18 C5
Grange La *YO23* 16 A5
Grange La *YO26* 16 B5
Grange St *YO10* 18 C5
Granger Ave *YO26* 16 D3
Granger Pl *YO26* 16 D3
Grantham Dr *YO26* 17 F4
Grants Ave *YO10* 26 A1
Granville Ter *YO10* 18 D4
Grape La **2** *YO1* 5 E2
Grasmere Dr *YO10* 19 G3
Grasmere Gro *YO30* 12 A4
Grassholme *YO24* 24 A2
Gray St *YO23* 18 A5
Grayshon Dr *YO26* 16 C2
Great N Way (N.Pop.) *YO26* 11 F5
Green, The (Dun.) *YO19* 21 H2
Green, The (Acomb) *YO26* 16 D4
Green, The (U.Pop.) *YO26* 10 C4
Green Cl *YO30* 12 B5
Green Dike (Wig.) *YO32* 7 G3
Green Dykes La *YO10* 19 E4
Green La *YO23* 25 F3
Green La (Acomb) *YO24* 17 E5
Green La (Clifton) *YO30* 12 A4
Green La Trd Est (Clifton) *YO30* 12 B4
Green Meadows *YO31* 13 H6
Green Sward *YO31* 13 H5
Greenacres (Hunt.) *YO32* 13 G1
Greencliffe Dr *YO30* 17 H1
Greencroft Ct (Dun.) *YO19* 21 H1
Greencroft La (Dun.) *YO19* 21 H2
Greenfield Pk Dr *YO31* 13 H6
Greengate (A.Bry.) *YO23* 23 F4
Greensborough Ave *YO26* 16 C2
Greenshaw Dr (Haxby) *YO32* 7 H3
Greenshaw Dr (Wig.) *YO32* 7 G2
Greenside (Dun.) *YO19* 21 H2
Greenside Cl (Dun.) *YO19* 21 H2
Greenside Wk (Dun.) *YO19* 21 H2
Greenway (Hunt.) *YO32* 13 G1
Greenway, The (Haxby) *YO32* 7 H4
Greenwich Cl **5** *YO30* 11 H2
Greenwood Gro *YO24* 23 H1
Gregory Cl (Skel.) *YO30* 6 B6
Gresley Ct *YO26* 16 C3
Greystoke Rd *YO30* 11 H4
Greystone Ct (Haxby) *YO32* 7 H5
Grimwith Garth **5** *YO30* 12 A3
Grosvenor Rd *YO30* 18 A1
Grosvenor Ter *YO30* 18 A1
Grove, The *YO24* 24 C3
Grove Gdns **2** (U.Pop.) *YO26* 10 C4
Grove Ter *YO24* 16 D4
Grove Ter La *YO31* 18 C1
Grove Vw *YO30* 17 H1
Groves Ct *YO31* 5 F1
Groves La *YO31* 5 F1
Guardian Ct *YO30* 12 B6
Guildhall, The *YO1* 4 D3

H

Haddon Cl *YO24* 16 D5
Hadrian Ave *YO10* 19 G4
Haleys Ter *YO31* 13 E5
Halifax Ct *YO30* 12 B4
Hall Pk (Hes.) *YO10* 19 G6
Hall Ri (Haxby) *YO32* 8 A2
Halladale Cl *YO24* 23 H2
Hallard Way (Stren.) *YO32* 9 G4
Hallcroft La (Cop.) *YO23* 22 A1
Hallfield Rd *YO31* 5 H2
Hambleton Ave *YO10* 19 H3
Hambleton Ter *YO31* 12 D6
Hambleton Vw **10** (Wig.) *YO32* 7 G1
Hambleton Way (Hunt.) *YO32* 13 G2
Hamilton Dr *YO24* 17 F5
Hamilton Dr E *YO24* 17 G5
Hamilton Dr W *YO24* 17 E5
Hamilton Way *YO24* 17 F5
Hammerton Cl *YO26* 16 C4
Hampden St *YO1* 4 D5
Handley Cl **3** *YO30* 12 B3
Hanover St E **6** *YO26* 17 G2
Hanover St W **4** *YO26* 17 G2
Hansom Pl **8** *YO31* 12 D6
Harcourt Cl (Bish.) *YO23* 25 E6
Harcourt St *YO31* 18 D2
Harden Cl *YO30* 12 A3
Harewood Cl *YO30* 11 G3
Harewood Cl (Wig.) *YO32* 7 G1
Harington Ave *YO10* 19 E3
Harlow Cl *YO24* 17 G5
Harlow Ct **3** (Stren.) *YO32* 9 F5
Harlow Rd *YO24* 17 G5
Harold Ct *YO24* 17 E4
Harrison St *YO31* 19 E1
Harrow Glade *YO30* 12 B4
Hartoft St *YO10* 18 C5
Haslemere Ct (Hunt.) *YO32* 13 F2
Hastings Cl *YO30* 12 B4
Hatfield Cl **3** *YO30* 11 H2
Hatfield Wk *YO24* 23 H1
Hatters Cl **5** (Cop.) *YO23* 22 B1
Haughton Rd *YO30* 12 D6
Haverah Ct **8** *YO30* 12 A4
Hawkshead Cl *YO24* 23 H1
Hawthorn Cl (N.Ears.) *YO32* 13 E2
Hawthorn Gro *YO31* 5 H1
Hawthorn Meadow **15** *YO30* 12 B5
Hawthorn Pl **1** (N.Ears.) *YO32* 13 F1
Hawthorn Spinney *YO31* 13 F2
Hawthorn St *YO31* 5 H1
Hawthorn Ter (N.Ears.) *YO32* 13 E2
Hawthorn Ter Cen (N.Ears.) *YO32* 13 E2
Hawthorn Ter N (N.Ears.) *YO32* 13 E1
Hawthorn Ter S (N.Ears.) *YO32* 13 E2
Hawthorne Ave (Haxby) *YO32* 8 A2
Hawthorne Cl (N.Pop.) *YO26* 10 C3
Haxby Moor Rd (Stren.) *YO32* 9 F3
Haxby Rd *YO31* 18 B1
Haxby Rd (N.Ears.) *YO32* 13 E4
Hayforth Cl **4** *YO30* 12 B3
Hazel Cl **2** (N.Ears.) *YO32* 13 E3
Hazel Garth *YO31* 19 G1
Hazelnut Gro *YO30* 12 B3
Hazelwood Ave *YO10* 20 A3
Headland Cl (Haxby) *YO32* 7 H2
Headley Cl *YO30* 12 B4
Healey Gro *YO31* 13 G5
Heath Cl *YO24* 17 G5
Heath Cft *YO10* 26 B2
Heath Moor Dr *YO10* 26 B1
Heath Ride (Stren.) *YO32* 9 H2
Heather Bk *YO10* 19 H3
Heather Cl (Hunt.) *YO32* 13 H1
Heather Cft *YO31* 13 F3
Heathfield Rd *YO10* 19 F4
Hebden Ri *YO26* 17 E4
Helmsdale *YO24* 23 H2
Helmsley Gro (Wig.) *YO32* 7 F2
Hemlock Ave *YO31* 13 F4
Hempland Ave *YO31* 19 E1
Hempland Dr *YO31* 13 H6
Hempland La *YO31* 13 H6
Hendon Garth *YO30* 12 B4
Herbert St **2** *YO10* 18 D4
Herberts Way *YO31* 13 G6
Herdsman Dr (Cop.) *YO23* 22 C1
Herdsman Rd *YO24* 24 B1
Herdwick Cl *YO30* 12 B4
Herman Wk *YO24* 24 A1
Heron Ave *YO24* 24 A1
Heron Ri (Hunt.) *YO32* 8 C6
Hesketh Bk *YO10* 19 H4
Heslin Cl **3** (Haxby) *YO32* 7 H3
Heslington Ct (Hes.) *YO10* 19 G6
Heslington Cft (Fulford) *YO10* 26 A1
Heslington La *YO10* 26 A2
Heslington Rd *YO10* 5 H6
Hessay Pl *YO26* 16 B4
Hetherton St *YO30* 4 B2
Hewley Ave *YO10* 19 E3
Heworth Grn *YO31* 5 G1
Heworth Hall Dr *YO31* 19 E1
Heworth Pl *YO31* 19 E1
Heworth Rd *YO31* 19 E1
Heworth Village *YO31* 19 E1
High Fld *YO10* 20 A3
High Newbiggin St **5** *YO31* 5 E1
High Oaks *YO31* 14 A6
High Ousegate *YO1* 5 E4
High Petergate *YO1* 4 D2
Highcliffe Ct *YO30* 17 H1
Highgrove Cl **4** *YO30* 11 H2
Highlands Ave (Stren.) *YO32* 9 G4

Highmoor Cl YO24 24 B1
Highmoor Rd YO24 24 B1
Highthorn Rd YO31 13 F3
Hilbeck Gro YO31 19 G1
Hilbra Ave (Haxby) YO32 8 A5
Hilda St YO10 18 D4
Hill St YO24 17 F4
Hill Vw YO31 14 B6
Hillary Garth **3** YO26 17 G3
Hillcrest Ave (N.Pop.) YO26 10 D3
Hillcrest Gdns YO24 17 G6
Hillsborough Ter **1** YO30 12 D6
Hinton Ave YO24 24 A1
Hob Moor Dr YO24 17 F5
Hob Moor Ter YO24 17 G6
Hobgate YO24 17 E4
Hobson Cl (Cop.) YO23 22 A3
Hodgson La (U.Pop.) YO26 10 B5
Holburns Cft (Hes.) YO10 19 F6
Holgate Br Gdns **2** YO24 17 H4
Holgate Lo Dr YO26 17 F3
Holgate Rd YO24 17 G4
Hollands Rd YO10 18 D6
Hollis Cres (Stren.) YO32 9 G5
Holly Bk Gro YO24 17 G5
Holly Bk Rd YO24 17 G5
Holly Ter **5** YO10 18 C6
Holly Tree Cft (Dun.) YO19 21 H1
Holly Tree La (Dun.) YO19 21 H1
Holly Tree La (Haxby) YO32 8 A3
Holmefield La YO10 19 F6
Holroyd Ave YO31 19 F2
Holtby La YO19 15 E3
Holyrood Dr YO30 11 G2
Homefield Cl (Cop.) YO23 22 A2
Homestead Cl (Hunt.) YO32 13 G4
Hope St YO10 5 G5
Hopgrove La N YO32 14 B2
Hopgrove La S YO32 14 C2
Hornbeam Cl YO30 12 C3
Horner St YO30 12 C6
Hornsey Garth (Wig.) YO32 7 H2
Horseman Ave (Cop.) YO23 22 A1
Horseman Cl (Cop.) YO23 22 A1
Horseman Dr (Cop.) YO23 22 A1
Horseman La (Cop.) YO23 22 A1
Horseshoe, The YO24 24 C2
Horsfield Way (Dun.) YO19 21 H1
Horsman Ave YO10 5 G6
Hospital Flds **6** YO10 18 C6
Hospital Flds Rd YO10 18 B6
Hospital Flds Ter **7** YO10 18 C6
Hospital La YO31 18 B1
Hotham Ave YO26 16 C5
Hothams Ct **11** YO1 5 F4
Houndsway YO24 23 H1
Howard Dr YO30 11 G3
Howard Link YO30 11 G3
Howard Rd (Stren.) YO32 9 G5
Howard St YO10 18 C5
Howe Hill Cl YO26 17 F3
Howe Hill Rd YO26 17 F3
Howe St **5** YO24 17 E4
Hubert St YO23 18 A6
Huby Ct **1** YO1 5 H5
Hudson Cres **4** YO30 12 B6
Hudson St **3** YO30 12 D6
Hudson Way (N.Pop.) YO26 11 F5
Hull Rd YO10 19 F4
Hull Rd (Dun.) YO19 21 E3
Humber Dr (Stren.) YO32 9 G5
Hungate YO1 5 F3
Hunt Ct YO1 5 F2
Hunters Cl (Dun.) YO19 21 F2
Hunters Cl **6** (Haxby) YO32 7 H3
Hunters Way YO24 24 D2
Hunterswood Way (Dun.) YO19 21 G2
Huntington Rd YO31 13 E6
Huntington Rd (Hunt.) YO32 13 F3
Huntsmans Wk YO24 16 D6
Hurricane Way YO30 11 H2
Hursts Yd YO1 5 G4
Hutton Cl (N.Pop.) YO26 10 D3
Hyrst Gro YO31 18 D1

I

Ikin Way (Hunt.) YO32 8 C6
Ilton Garth YO30 12 B3
Ingleborough Ave YO10 19 G3
Ingleton Wk YO31 19 F2
Ingram Ave YO30 12 C5
Ings La (N.Pop.) YO26 11 E4
Ings Vw YO30 11 G3
Ings Way YO30 12 A5
Inman Ter YO26 17 E3
Intake Ave YO30 12 D6
Intake La (Dun.) YO19 21 H2
Invicta Ct YO24 23 H1
Irvine Way YO24 23 H2
Irwin Ave YO31 18 D1
Iver Cl YO26 16 D2
Ivy Pl (N.Ears.) YO32 13 E2

J

Jackson St YO31 18 C1
Jacobi Cl YO30 12 B6
James Backhouse Pl YO24 17 F4
James Nicholson Link YO30 12 B3
James St YO10 5 H3
Jamieson Ter YO23 18 A6
Jasmine Cl (N.Ears.) YO32 13 E3
Jaywick Cl (Stren.) YO32 9 H2
Jedwell Cl **2** (N.Ears.) YO32 13 E1
Jennifer Gro YO24 17 G5
Jervis Rd YO24 24 B1
Jewbury YO31 5 F2
Jockey La (Hunt.) YO32 14 A4
John St YO31 18 D1
Jorvik Cl YO26 16 D2
Jubbergate YO1 5 E3
Jubilee Ter YO26 17 G2
Judges Ct **10** YO1 4 D3
Julia Ave (Hunt.) YO32 14 A3
Juniper Cl (N.Ears.) YO32 13 E3
Jute Rd YO26 16 C2

K

Kathryn Ave (Hunt.) YO32 13 H3
Keats Cl **1** YO30 12 A5
Keble Cl (Bish.) YO23 25 F6
Keble Dr (Bish.) YO23 25 E6
Keble Pk Cres (Bish.) YO23 25 E6
Keble Pk N (Bish.) YO23 25 E6
Keble Pk S (Bish.) YO23 25 E6
Keeper's Way (Dun.) YO19 21 H1
Keith Ave (Hunt.) YO32 13 H1
Keldale (Haxby) YO32 8 B1
Kempton Cl YO24 17 E6
Kendal Cl (Dun.) YO19 21 H1
Kendrew Cl (Hunt.) YO32 13 G2
Kenlay Cl **8** (N.Ears.) YO32 13 E1
Kennedy Dr (Haxby) YO32 8 A2
Kenrick Pl YO26 16 C2
Kensal Ri YO10 18 C5
Kensington Ct (Drin.) YO24 24 D1
Kensington Rd YO30 11 G3
Kensington St YO23 18 A6
Kent St YO10 5 G6
Kentmere Dr YO30 11 H4
Kerrside **6** YO30 11 H5
Kerver La (Dun.) YO19 21 H1
Kestrel Wd Way YO31 13 F3
Keswick Way (Hunt.) YO32 8 C6
Kettlestring La YO30 12 B3
Kexby Ave YO10 19 E4
Key Way (Fulford) YO19 26 A4
Kilburn Rd YO10 18 C5
Kimberlows Wds Hill YO10 19 H4
Kinbrace Dr YO24 23 H2
King St **18** YO1 5 E4
Kingfisher Cl (Hunt.) YO32 8 C6
Kings Acre YO31 19 G1
Kings Ct **5** YO1 5 E3
Kings Sq **4** YO1 5 E3
Kings Staith YO1 5 E4
Kingsclere (Hunt.) YO32 8 C6
Kingsland Ter YO26 17 G2
Kingsmoor Rd (St.For.) YO32 15 F1
Kingsthorpe YO24 17 E5
Kingsway N YO30 12 C6
Kingsway W YO24 17 E5
Kingswood Gro YO24 17 E4
Kir Cres YO24 16 D5
Kirk Vw YO26 16 D4
Kirkcroft (Wig.) YO32 7 H3
Kirkdale Rd YO10 20 A3
Kirkham Ave YO31 13 E5
Kirklands (Stren.) YO32 9 G4
Kirkstone Dr YO31 19 F1
Kirkwell (Bish.) YO23 25 E5
Kitchener St YO31 13 E6
Kitemere Pl YO24 23 H1
Knapton Cl (Stren.) YO32 9 G5
Knapton La YO26 16 C3
Knavesmire Cres YO23 18 A6
Knavesmire Rd YO23 17 H5
Knoll, The YO24 16 C6
Kyle Way (N.Pop.) YO26 11 E5
Kyme St YO1 4 D5

L

Laburnum Garth YO31 13 G5
Lady Hamilton Gdns YO24 17 E5
Lady Hewley's Cotts **3** YO1 5 F3
Lady Mill Garth **6** YO30 12 C5
Lady Peckitts Yd **13** YO1 5 E4
Lady Rd YO30 12 C6
Lady Wortley Pl (Midd.) YO23 25 G3
Ladysmith Ms **5** (Stren.) YO32 9 F4
Lakeside Ct **1** YO24 24 D1
Lakeside Gdns (Stren.) YO32 9 H2
Lambert Ct YO1 4 D5
Lamel St YO10 19 F4
Lamplugh Cres (Bish.) YO23 25 F6
Lancar Cl (Wig.) YO32 7 F2
Lancaster Way YO30 12 B4
Landalewood Rd **3** YO30 12 A3
Landau Cl **4** YO30 12 A5
Landing La YO26 17 F2
Landing La (Haxby) YO32 8 C2
Landings, The (Haxby) YO32 8 B2
Landsdown Way (Haxby) YO32 8 B2
Lang Ave YO10 19 F3
Lang Rd YO23 24 D5
Lang Rd (Hunt.) YO32 8 C6
Langdale Ave YO31 19 F1
Langholme Dr YO26 16 D1
Langley Ct (Hunt.) YO32 8 C6
Langsett Gro YO30 12 A2
Langton Ct (Stren.) YO32 9 F5
Langwith La (Hes.) YO10 27 G2
Lansdowne Ter YO10 18 D4
Lanshaw Cft YO30 12 A4
Larch Way (Haxby) YO32 8 A1
Larchfield YO31 14 A6
Larkfield Cl (Cop.) YO23 22 A1
Lasenby Cl **1** (N.Ears.) YO32 13 E1
Lastingham Ter YO10 18 C5
Lavender Gro YO26 17 F2
Lawnswood Dr YO30 12 A5
Lawnway YO31 13 H6
Lawrence St YO10 5 H5
Lawson Rd YO24 24 D3
Layerthorpe YO31 5 G2
Layerthorpe Br YO31 5 G2
Lea Way (Hunt.) YO32 13 H1
Lead Mill La YO1 5 F5
Leadley Cft (Cop.) YO23 22 A3
Leake St YO10 5 H5
Learmans Way (Cop.) YO23 22 C1
Leeman Rd YO26 4 A3
Leeside YO24 24 B1
Leicester Way **6** YO1 5 F5
Leighton Cft YO30 12 A4
Lendal YO1 4 D3
Lendal Br YO1 4 D3
Lerecroft Rd YO24 24 B1
Lesley Ave YO10 26 A1
Leven Rd YO24 24 B2
Levisham St YO10 18 C5
Leyes, The YO10 19 H3

Leyfield Cl **1** (Stren.) *YO32* 9 F4
Leyland Rd *YO31* 19 F2
Library Sq **7** *YO1* 4 D2
Lichfield Ct *YO23* 18 A6
Lidgett Gro *YO26* 16 C1
Lilac Ave *YO10* 19 G4
Lilac Gro (N.Ears.) *YO32* 13 E1
Lilbourne Dr *YO30* 12 B5
Lilling Ave *YO31* 13 F5
Lime Ave *YO31* 13 G6
Lime Garth (U.Pop.) *YO26* 10 C4
Lime Tree Ave (N.Ears.) *YO32* 13 E2
Lime Tree Ms (Dun.) *YO19* 21 H1
Limes, The (St.For.) *YO32* 15 F1
Lincoln St *YO26* 17 G2
Lindale *YO24* 24 A2
Linden Cl (Hunt.) *YO32* 8 C6
Linden Gro *YO30* 12 A5
Lindley Rd *YO30* 12 A4
Lindley St *YO24* 17 G4
Lindley Wd Gro **7** *YO30* 11 H2
Lindsey Ave *YO26* 17 E3
Lingfield Cres *YO24* 17 G6
Link, The *YO10* 26 A1
Link, The (Cop.) *YO23* 22 A1
Link Ave *YO30* 12 D5
Link Rd *YO32* 13 E3
Linley Ave (Haxby) *YO32* 8 B2
Linnet Way *YO24* 24 A1
Linton Rd (N.Pop.) *YO26* 10 D4
Linton St *YO26* 17 F2
Lister Way *YO30* 12 B6
Little Ave *YO30* 12 C5
Little Garth (N.Pop.) *YO26* 10 C3
Little Hallfield Rd *YO31* 5 H2
Little La (Haxby) *YO32* 8 A2
Little Meadows (Haxby) *YO32* 8 A3
Little Shambles *YO1* 5 E3
Little Stonegate *YO1* 4 D3
Littlefield Cl (N.Pop.) *YO26* 10 C3
Livingstone St *YO26* 17 G2
Lloyd Cl (Hes.) *YO10* 19 G6
Lochrin Pl *YO26* 16 C3
Lock Ho La (Ears.) *YO32* 8 C3
Lockey Cft (Wig.) *YO32* 7 H3
Lockwood St *YO31* 5 F1
Long Cl La *YO10* 5 G5
Long Furrow (Haxby) *YO32* 7 H3
Long Ridge Dr (U.Pop.) *YO26* 10 D4
Long Ridge La *YO26* 10 C4
Longcroft (Wig.) *YO32* 7 H1
Longfield Ter *YO30* 4 B2
Longwood Link *YO30* 11 H2
Longwood Rd *YO30* 12 A2
Lord Mayors Wk *YO31* 5 E1
Lords Moor La (Stren.) *YO32* 9 H3
Loriners Dr (Cop.) *YO23* 22 B1
Lorne St *YO23* 18 A6
Lorrenger La (A.Bry.) *YO23* 23 F2
Love La *YO10* 25 G1
Love La *YO24* 17 H5
Lovel Ho *YO24* 24 B1
Lovell St *YO23* 18 B5
Low Flds Dr *YO24* 16 D5
Low Grn (Cop.) *YO23* 22 B2
Low La (Hes.) *YO10* 26 D1
Low Mill Cl *YO10* 20 A4
Low Moor Ave *YO10* 26 B2
Low Ousegate *YO1* 4 D4
Low Petergate *YO1* 5 E2
Low Poppleton La *YO26* 11 E6
Lowcroft (Stren.) *YO32* 9 F4
Lower Darnborough St *YO23* 5 E6
Lower Ebor St *YO23* 18 B5
Lower Friargate **17** *YO1* 5 E4
Lower Priory St *YO1* 4 C5
Loweswater Rd **11** *YO30* 11 H4
Lowfield Dr (Haxby) *YO32* 8 A1
Lowfield La (Knapton) *YO26* 16 A3
Lowick *YO24* 24 A2
Lown Hill *YO24* 16 D5
Lowther St *YO31* 18 B1
Lowther Ter *YO24* 4 A5
Loxley Cl *YO30* 12 A3
Lucas Ave *YO30* 12 D5
Lucombe Way (N.Ears.) *YO32* 13 E1
Lumley Rd *YO30* 12 C6
Lund Cl (Wig.) *YO32* 7 G3
Lundy Cl **2** *YO30* 12 B4
Lycett Rd *YO24* 24 D3
Lydham Ct *YO24* 24 A1
Lyndale Ave *YO10* 19 H4
Lynden Way *YO24* 17 E4
Lynwood Ave (Cop.) *YO23* 22 A1
Lynwood Cl (Stren.) *YO32* 9 F4
Lynwood Vw (Cop.) *YO23* 22 A1
Lysander Cl *YO30* 12 B3

M

Maclagan Rd (Bish.) *YO23* 24 D5
Magnolia Gro **3** (N.Ears.) *YO32* 13 E3
Maida Gro *YO10* 18 C5
Main Ave *YO31* 19 E2
Main St (Fulford) *YO10* 25 H2
Main St (Hes.) *YO10* 19 F6
Main St (A.Bry.) *YO23* 22 D4
Main St (A.Rich.) *YO23* 22 B5
Main St (Bish.) *YO23* 25 E5
Main St (Cop.) *YO23* 22 A2
Main St (Knapton) *YO26* 16 B2
Main St (N.Pop.) *YO26* 10 B3
Main St (U.Pop.) *YO26* 10 C3
Malbys Gro (Cop.) *YO23* 22 B2
Malham Gro *YO31* 19 G2
Mallard Way (Haxby) *YO32* 8 B2
Mallory Cl **6** (N.Ears.) *YO32* 13 E1
Malt Shovel Ct **9** *YO1* 5 F4
Malton Ave *YO31* 18 D1
Malton Rd *YO31* 13 G5
Malton Rd *YO32* 14 A4
Malton Way *YO30* 12 A5
Malvern Ave *YO26* 17 E3
Malvern Cl (Hunt.) *YO32* 8 D6
Mancroft (Haxby) *YO32* 7 H4
Manley Cl **7** (N.Ears.) *YO32* 13 E1
Manor Beeches, The (Dun.) *YO19* 21 G1
Manor Cl (U.Pop.) *YO26* 10 C5
Manor Ct (U.Pop.) *YO26* 10 C4
Manor Ct **1** (Hunt.) *YO32* 8 C5
Manor Dr (Dun.) *YO19* 21 G2
Manor Dr N *YO26* 17 E3
Manor Dr S *YO26* 17 E3
Manor Fm Cl (Cop.) *YO23* 22 A2
Manor Garth (Wig.) *YO32* 7 G3
Manor Heath (Cop.) *YO23* 22 A1
Manor La *YO30* 11 G3
Manor Pk Cl *YO30* 11 H3
Manor Pk Gro *YO30* 11 G3
Manor Pk Rd *YO30* 11 G3
Manor Way *YO30* 11 H3
Mansfield St *YO31* 5 G2
Manthorpe Wk *YO26* 17 F3
Maple Ave (Bish.) *YO23* 25 E6
Maple Ct (N.Ears.) *YO32* 13 E2
Maple Gro *YO10* 18 C6
Maplewood Paddock *YO24* 16 D6
March St *YO31* 18 C1
Margaret Philipson Ct **2** *YO1* 5 F2
Margaret St *YO10* 5 G5
Marjorie Waite Ct **5** *YO30* 12 C6
Market St *YO1* 5 E4
Markham Cres *YO31* 18 B1
Markham St *YO31* 18 B1
Marlborough Cl **1** *YO30* 11 G2
Marlborough Gro *YO10* 18 C5
Marmian Dr (St.For.) *YO32* 15 F1
Marsden Pk *YO30* 12 B3
Marston Ave *YO26* 16 C4
Marston Cres *YO26* 16 C4
Marten Cl **11** *YO30* 12 B5
Martin Cheeseman Ct *YO24* 24 A1
Marygate *YO30* 4 C2
Marygate La *YO30* 4 C2
Matmer Ct *YO10* 19 E4
Mattison Way *YO24* 17 F5
Mayfield Gro *YO24* 24 D1
Maythorn Rd *YO31* 13 F3
McHugh Ct **1** (Hes.) *YO10* 26 D1
Meadlands *YO31* 19 G1
Meadow Ct *YO24* 24 C1
Meadow La (Haxby) *YO32* 8 A3
Meadow Way *YO31* 13 G6
Meadow Way (Hunt.) *YO32* 13 G1
Meadowbeck Cl *YO10* 19 G3
Meadowfields Dr *YO31* 13 E3
Meadows, The **1** (Skel.) *YO30* 6 A6
Melander Cl *YO26* 16 C3
Melander Gdns (Haxby) *YO32* 8 A4
Melbourne St *YO10* 18 C5
Melcombe Ave (Stren.) *YO32* 9 G4
Melrose Cl *YO31* 19 F2
Melrose Ct *YO31* 19 E3
Melrosegate *YO10* 19 E4
Melrosegate *YO31* 19 E2
Melroses Yd *YO1* 5 G4
Melton Ave *YO30* 12 A5
Melton Dr (Bish.) *YO23* 25 E6
Melton Dr *YO30* 12 A5
Melwood Gro *YO26* 16 C2
Mendip Cl (Hunt.) *YO32* 8 C6
Merchant Gate *YO1* 5 F4
Merchant Way (Cop.) *YO23* 22 B1
Merlin Covert **5** *YO31* 13 G2
Metcalfe La *YO19* 19 H2
Micklegate *YO1* 4 C4
Micklegate Bar *YO1* 4 B5
Middle Banks (Wig.) *YO32* 7 G2
Middlecroft Dr (Stren.) *YO32* 9 F4
Middlecroft Gro (Stren.) *YO32* 9 G4
Middleham Ave *YO31* 13 F5
Middlethorpe Dr *YO24* 24 C2
Middlethorpe Gro *YO24* 24 D2
Middleton Rd *YO24* 17 E5
Midway Ave (N.Pop.) *YO26* 10 D4
Mildred Gro *YO24* 17 G5
Milford Way (Haxby) *YO32* 8 A4
Mill Gates *YO26* 16 D1
Mill Hill Dr (Hunt.) *YO32* 13 G1
Mill La (A.Bry.) *YO23* 23 F5
Mill La *YO31* 18 D1
Mill La (Wig.) *YO32* 7 F2
Mill Mt *YO24* 4 A6
Mill Mt Ct *YO24* 4 A6
Mill St *YO1* 5 F5
Millers Cft (Cop.) *YO23* 22 B1
Millfield Ave *YO10* 19 E4
Millfield Gdns (N.Pop.) *YO26* 10 D3
Millfield La *YO10* 19 F4
Millfield La (N.Pop.) *YO26* 11 E5
Millfield Rd *YO23* 18 A5
Milner St *YO24* 17 E4
Milson Gro *YO10* 19 F4
Milton Carr *YO30* 12 A4
Milton St *YO10* 19 E4
Minchin Cl *YO30* 12 C5
Minster Ave *YO31* 13 G3
Minster Cl (Wig.) *YO32* 7 H2
Minster Ct **8** *YO1* 5 E1
Minster Gates **1** *YO1* 5 E2
Minster Vw (Wig.) *YO32* 7 H3
Minster Yd *YO1* 5 E2
Minter Cl *YO24* 16 C6
Mistral Ct *YO31* 13 E6
Mitchels La *YO10* 26 B1
Miterdale *YO24* 24 A2
Moat Fld *YO10* 19 H3
Moatside Ct *YO31* 5 E1
Moiser Cl **10** (N.Ears.) *YO32* 13 E1
Monk Ave *YO31* 13 G6
Monk Bar Ct **1** *YO1* 5 F2
Monk Br *YO31* 18 C1
Monkgate *YO31* 5 F1
Monkgate Cloisters *YO31* 5 F1
Monks Cross Dr (Hunt.) *YO32* 14 A3
Monks Cross Link *YO32* 9 E6
Monkton Rd *YO31* 13 F5
Montague Rd (Bish.) *YO23* 25 E6
Montague St *YO23* 18 A6
Montague Wk (U.Pop.) *YO26* 10 C3
Montrose Ave *YO31* 13 E5
Moor Gro *YO24* 24 C1
Moor La (Murton) *YO19* 20 C1
Moor La (A.Bry.) *YO23* 23 H3

Moor La (Bish.) *YO23*	24	D6
Moor La (Cop.) *YO23*	22	A3
Moor La *YO24*	24	C2
Moor La (Haxby) *YO32*	7	H1
Moor La (Stren.) *YO32*	9	G4
Moor Lea Ave *YO24*	24	C1
Moor Way (Hunt.) *YO32*	13	H1
Moorcroft Rd *YO24*	24	B3
Moore Ave *YO10*	19	G3
Moorgarth Ave *YO24*	17	G5
Moorgate *YO24*	17	E4
Moorland Gdns (Cop.) *YO23*	22	A3
Moorland Garth (Stren.) *YO32*	9	F3
Moorland Rd *YO10*	25	H1
Moorlands Flds *YO10*	26	A1
Moorlands Rd (Skel.) *YO30*	6	B5
Morehall Cl *YO30*	12	A3
Morrell Ct *YO24*	23	H1
Morritt Cl *YO31*	13	G4
Moss St *YO23*	4	B6
Mount, The *YO24*	4	A6
Mount Ephraim *YO24*	4	A5
Mount Par *YO24*	4	A6
Mount Vale *YO24*	17	H5
Mount Vale Dr *YO24*	17	H5
Mowbray Dr *YO26*	16	D3
Muirfield Way *YO26*	16	C2
Mulberry Ct (Hunt.) *YO32*	8	C5
Mulberry Dr (Haxby) *YO32*	8	A1
Mulwith Cl *YO31*	19	F1
Muncastergate *YO31*	13	F6
Murray St *YO24*	17	G4
Murrough Wilson Pl *YO31*	12	D6
Murton Garth (Murton) *YO19*	20	C1
Murton La (Murton) *YO19*	20	C1
Murton Way *YO19*	20	B2
Museum St *YO1*	4	C3
Myrtle Ave (Bish.) *YO23*	25	F6
N		
Naburn La *YO19*	25	G5
Nairn Cl *YO24*	24	A3
Nalton Cl (Cop.) *YO23*	22	A3
Navigation Rd *YO1*	5	G4
Nelson St *YO31*	18	C1
Nelsons La *YO24*	17	G6
Nessgate *YO1*	5	E4
Nether Hornpot La **21** *YO1*	5	E3
Nether Way (N.Pop.) *YO26*	10	C3
Nether Way (U.Pop.) *YO26*	10	C3
Netherwindings (Haxby) *YO32*	8	C2
Netherwoods (Stren.) *YO32*	9	G3
Neville Dr (Bish.) *YO23*	25	E6
Neville St *YO31*	18	C1
Neville Ter *YO31*	18	C1
Nevinson Gro *YO10*	26	B1
Nevis Way *YO24*	23	H2
New Forge Ct (Haxby) *YO32*	8	C2
New La (Bish.) *YO23*	24	D5
New La *YO24*	17	F4
New La (Hunt.) *YO32*	13	G3
New St *YO1*	4	D3
New Wk *YO10*	5	E6
New Wk Ter *YO10*	18	C5
Newborough St *YO30*	18	A1
Newbury Ave *YO24*	17	E6
Newby Ter **4** *YO31*	12	D6
Newdale (Haxby) *YO32*	8	B1
Newgate **7** *YO1*	5	E3
Newland Pk Cl *YO10*	19	E4
Newland Pk Dr *YO10*	19	F4
Newlands Dr *YO26*	16	C1
Newlands Rd (Bish.) *YO23*	24	D5
Newton Ter *YO1*	4	D5
Newton Way (Stren.) *YO32*	9	G5
Nicholas Gdns *YO10*	19	E4
Nicholas St *YO10*	18	D4
Nidd Cl (N.Pop.) *YO26*	11	E5
Nidd Gro *YO24*	24	C1
Nigel Gro *YO24*	17	G5
Nightingale Cl (Hunt.) *YO32*	13	F4
Ninth Ave *YO31*	19	E2
Norfolk St *YO23*	18	B5
Norman Dr *YO26*	16	C1
Norman St **5** *YO10*	19	F4
North Eastern Ter *YO24*	24	D1
North La *YO24*	24	C1
North La (Haxby) *YO32*	8	A2
North La (Hunt.) *YO32*	8	C6
North Moor (Hunt.) *YO32*	13	H1
North Moor Gdns (Hunt.) *YO32*	13	G1
North Moor Rd (Hunt.) *YO32*	8	C6
North Par *YO30*	4	B1
North St *YO1*	4	D4
Northcote Ave *YO24*	17	F4
Northcroft (Haxby) *YO32*	8	B2
Northfield La (A.Bry.) *YO23*	23	E3
Northfield La (U.Pop.) *YO26*	16	A1
Northfield Ter *YO24*	24	C1
Northfields (Stren.) *YO32*	9	H2
Northlands Ave **1** (Ears.) *YO32*	8	C4
Northolme Dr *YO30*	11	H5
Norway Dr *YO10*	25	H1
Nunmill St *YO23*	18	B5
Nunnery La *YO23*	4	B5
Nunthorpe Ave *YO23*	18	A5
Nunthorpe Cres *YO23*	18	A6
Nunthorpe Dr *YO23*	18	B5
Nunthorpe Gdns *YO23*	18	B5
Nunthorpe Gro *YO23*	18	A6
Nunthorpe Rd *YO23*	4	C6
Nunthorpe Vw *YO23*	18	B6
Nursery Ct (N.Pop.) *YO26*	10	D3
Nursery Dr *YO24*	17	F4
Nursery Gdns *YO10*	19	H4
Nursery Rd (N.Pop.) *YO26*	10	D4
O		
Oak Glade *YO31*	13	G3
Oak Ri *YO24*	16	D4
Oak St *YO26*	17	F2
Oak Tree Cl (Stren.) *YO32*	9	G5
Oak Tree Gro (N.Ears.) *YO32*	13	E3
Oak Tree La (Haxby) *YO32*	7	H4
Oak Tree Way (Stren.) *YO32*	9	G4
Oakdale Rd *YO30*	12	A3
Oaken Gro (Haxby) *YO32*	8	A1
Oakhill Cres (Stren.) *YO32*	9	F5
Oakland Ave *YO31*	13	G6
Oakland Dr *YO31*	13	H6
Oaklands (Stren.) *YO32*	9	G4
Oaks, The **11** (N.Ears.) *YO32*	13	E1
Oakville St *YO31*	13	E6
Ogleforth *YO1*	5	E2
Old Coppice (Haxby) *YO32*	8	C2
Old Dike Lands (Haxby) *YO32*	7	H3
Old Highway, The **3** (Stren.) *YO32*	9	G5
Old Moor La *YO24*	24	C2
Old Orchard (Haxby) *YO32*	8	A3
Old Orchard, The (Fulford) *YO10*	26	A2
Old Sch Ct **4** (U.Pop.) *YO26*	10	C4
Old Village, The (Hunt.) *YO32*	8	C6
Oldman Ct *YO24*	24	A1
Orchard, The (Bish.) *YO23*	25	E6
Orchard Cl *YO24*	17	F6
Orchard Cotts **1** (Dun.) *YO19*	21	H1
Orchard Gdns *YO31*	13	F3
Orchard Garth (Cop.) *YO23*	22	B1
Orchard Paddock (Haxby) *YO32*	8	A3
Orchard Rd (U.Pop.) *YO26*	10	C4
Orchard Vw (Skel.) *YO30*	6	A6
Orchard Way *YO24*	24	C1
Orchard Way (Stren.) *YO32*	9	G3
Ordnance La *YO10*	18	C6
Oriel Gro *YO30*	12	B5
Orrin Cl *YO24*	24	A2
Osbaldwick La *YO10*	19	G3
Osbaldwick Link Rd *YO10*	20	A3
Osbaldwick Link Rd *YO19*	20	A3
Osbaldwick Village *YO10*	19	H3
Osbourne Dr **6** *YO30*	11	H2
Osmington Gdns **6** (Stren.) *YO32*	9	F4
Osprey Cl *YO24*	23	H1
Ostlers Cl **2** (Cop.) *YO23*	22	C1
Ostman Rd *YO26*	16	C2
Otterwood Bk *YO24*	16	C6
Otterwood La *YO24*	16	C6
Ouse Acres *YO26*	17	E2
Ouse Br *YO1*	4	D4
Ouse Lea *YO30*	12	B6
Ouseburn Ave *YO26*	16	C1
Ousecliffe Gdns *YO30*	17	H1
Outgang, The (Hes.) *YO10*	26	D1
Outgang La (Osb.) *YO19*	20	A2
Overdale Cl *YO24*	24	B1
Ovington Ter *YO23*	18	A5
Owlwood Ct (Dun.) *YO19*	21	G2
Owlwood La (Dun.) *YO19*	21	G2
Owston Ave *YO10*	19	F4
Ox Calder Cl (Dun.) *YO19*	21	H2
Ox Carr La (Stren.) *YO32*	9	G5
Oxclose La (Hes.) *YO10*	27	G1
Oxford St *YO24*	4	A5
P		
Paddock, The *YO26*	16	D1
Paddock Cl (A.Rich.) *YO23*	22	A4
Paddock Cl (Cop.) *YO23*	22	A2
Paddock Way *YO26*	16	D1
Palace Vw (Fulford) *YO10*	25	H3
Palmer La *YO1*	5	F3
Parade Ct *YO31*	19	E1
Paragon St *YO10*	5	G6
Park Ave (N.Ears.) *YO32*	8	A6
Park Cl (Skel.) *YO30*	11	E1
Park Ct *YO31*	19	F2
Park Cres *YO31*	18	C1
Park Est (Haxby) *YO32*	8	A3
Park Gate (Stren.) *YO32*	9	H2
Park Gro *YO31*	18	C1
Park La (Holgate) *YO24*	17	G4
Park St *YO24*	4	B6
Parker Ave *YO26*	16	C5
Parkland Way (Haxby) *YO32*	8	A3
Parkside Cl *YO24*	17	F4
Parliament St *YO1*	5	E3
Paston Wk *YO23*	4	D6
Pasture Cl (Skel.) *YO30*	6	A6
Pasture Cl (Stren.) *YO32*	9	G5
Pasture Fm Cl (Fulford) *YO10*	25	H3
Pasture La *YO31*	14	A5
Pastures, The *YO24*	24	C1
Pately Pl *YO26*	17	E3
Patrick Pool **6** *YO1*	5	E3
Patterdale Dr *YO30*	11	H4
Pavement *YO1*	5	E4
Paver La *YO1*	5	G4
Pear Tree Ave (U.Pop.) *YO26*	10	C3
Pear Tree Cl (Hunt.) *YO32*	13	G1
Pear Tree Ct **5** *YO1*	5	F2
Pear Tree La (Dun.) *YO19*	21	G2
Peasholme Grn *YO1*	5	F3
Peckitt St *YO1*	5	E5
Peel Cl (Hes.) *YO10*	19	F6
Peel St **4** *YO1*	5	G5
Pelham Pl (Stren.) *YO32*	9	F5
Pembroke St *YO30*	12	C6
Penleys Ct **8** *YO31*	18	C1
Penleys Gro St *YO31*	18	C1
Pennine Cl (Hunt.) *YO32*	13	G1
Penny La Ct **4** *YO1*	5	F2
Pentire Cl **1** *YO30*	12	B4
Pentland Dr (Hunt.) *YO32*	13	G1
Penyghent Ave *YO31*	19	F2
Peppercorn Cl **1** *YO26*	17	F3
Percys La *YO1*	5	G4
Peter Hill Dr *YO30*	12	B5
Peter La *YO1*	5	E4
Petercroft Cl (Dun.) *YO19*	21	H1
Petercroft La (Dun.) *YO19*	21	H1
Petersway *YO30*	18	A1
Pheasant Dr *YO24*	23	H2
Philadelphia Ter *YO23*	18	A5
Piccadilly *YO1*	5	F4
Pike Hills Mt (Cop.) *YO23*	22	A1
Pilgrim St **2** *YO31*	18	B1
Pinelands (Haxby) *YO32*	8	A4
Pinelands Way *YO10*	19	H4
Pinewood Gro **3** *YO31*	13	F4

Pinewood Hill *YO10* 19 H4
Pinfold Ct **3** *YO30* 12 B6
Plantation Dr *YO26* 16 D1
Plantation Gro *YO26* 16 D1
Plantation Way (Wig.) *YO32* 7 G2
Ploughlands (Haxby) *YO32* 7 H4
Ploughmans Cl (Cop.) *YO23* 22 B1
Ploughman's La (Haxby) *YO32* 7 H4
Plumer Ave *YO31* 19 F2
Pollard Cl (Hunt.) *YO32* 13 F2
Poplar Gro (N.Ears.) *YO32* 13 E2
Poplar St *YO26* 17 F2
Poppleton Hall Gdns (N.Pop.) *YO26* 10 D2
Poppleton Rd *YO24* 17 F3
Poppleton Rd *YO26* 17 F3
Portal Rd *YO26* 16 C1
Portisham Pl (Stren.) *YO32* 9 F4
Portland St *YO31* 4 D1
Postern Cl *YO23* 5 E6
Potters Dr **4** (Cop.) *YO23* 22 B1
Pottery La *YO31* 13 F6
Precentors Ct *YO1* 4 D2
Prestwick Ct *YO26* 16 C2
Price St **2** *YO23* 4 C6
Prices La *YO23* 4 D6
Princess Rd (Stren.) *YO32* 9 G3
Priors Wk *YO26* 17 E1
Priory St *YO1* 4 C5
Priory Wd Way *YO31* 13 G3
Prospect Ter *YO1* 4 C5
Prospect Ter (Fulford) *YO10* 25 H3
Pulleyn Dr *YO24* 17 G6

Q

Quaker Grn *YO24* 24 A2
Quant Ms *YO10* 19 G4
Queen Annes Rd *YO30* 4 B1
Queen St *YO24* 4 B4
Queen Victoria St *YO23* 18 A6
Queens Staith **19** *YO1* 4 D4
Queens Staith Ms **8** *YO1* 4 D5
Queens Staith Rd **20** *YO1* 4 D4
Queenswood Gro *YO24* 17 E5

R

Radley Ct **2** (Stren.) *YO32* 9 F5
Railway Ter *YO24* 17 H3
Railway Vw *YO24* 24 C1
Rainsborough Way *YO30* 12 B5
Ramsay Cl *YO31* 18 C1
Ramsey Ave (Bish.) *YO23* 25 E6
Ratcliffe Ct (Skel.) *YO30* 6 B6
Ratcliffe St *YO30* 12 C6
Raven Gro *YO26* 16 D3
Rawcliffe Ave *YO30* 12 A5
Rawcliffe Cl *YO30* 11 H3
Rawcliffe Cft *YO30* 11 G3
Rawcliffe Dr *YO30* 12 A5
Rawcliffe Gro *YO30* 12 A6
Rawcliffe Landing (Skel.) *YO30* 11 F2
Rawcliffe La *YO30* 12 A5
Rawcliffe Village *YO30* 11 H2
Rawcliffe Way *YO30* 11 H3
Rawdon Ave *YO10* 19 E3
Raynard Ct *YO24* 24 A1
Rectory Gdns *YO23* 18 A6
Redcoat Way *YO24* 23 H1
Redeness St *YO31* 5 H2
Redman Cl *YO10* 25 H1
Redmayne Sq **1** (Stren.) *YO32* 9 H2
Redmires Cl *YO30* 12 B3
Redthorn Dr *YO31* 13 G4
Redwood Dr (Haxby) *YO32* 7 H2
Reeves, The *YO24* 16 D6
Regency Ms (Drin.) *YO24* 24 D1
Regent St *YO10* 5 H6
Regents Ct **11** *YO26* 17 G2
Reginald Gro *YO23* 18 B6
Reighton Ave *YO30* 12 A5
Reighton Dr *YO30* 12 A4
Renfrew Grn (Stren.) *YO32* 9 H2
Renshaw Gdns *YO26* 17 F3
Reygate Gro (Cop.) *YO23* 22 B2
Ribstone Gro *YO31* 19 G1
Richardson St *YO23* 18 B5
Richmond St *YO31* 5 H2
Ridgeway *YO26* 16 C4
Ringstone Rd *YO30* 12 A2
Ripley Gro (Wig.) *YO32* 7 H1
Rishworth Gro *YO30* 12 A3
Rivelin Way *YO30* 12 A3
River St **6** *YO23* 5 E6
Riversdale (Haxby) *YO32* 8 C1
Riverside Cres (Hunt.) *YO32* 8 C5
Riverside Gdns (N.Pop.) *YO26* 10 C3
Riverside Wk *YO1* 4 D3
Riverside Wk (N.Pop.) *YO26* 10 C3
Riverside Wk (Stren.) *YO32* 9 F4
Riversvale Dr (N.Pop.) *YO26* 10 C3
Robin Gro *YO24* 17 G4
Robinson Ct **4** *YO1* 5 G4
Robinson Dr *YO24* 16 C5
Roche Ave *YO31* 13 F5
Rockingham Ave *YO31* 19 F2
Rogers Ct *YO24* 24 A1
Roland Ct (Hunt.) *YO32* 13 F2
Rolston Ave *YO31* 13 F3
Ropers Ct (Cop.) *YO23* 22 C1
Ropewalk, The *YO31* 5 H2
Rose St *YO31* 12 D6
Rose Tree Gro (N.Ears.) *YO32* 13 E1
Roseberry Gro **9** *YO30* 12 A2
Rosebery St *YO26* 17 G1
Rosecomb Way (Haxby) *YO32* 8 A4
Rosecroft Way *YO30* 11 H5
Rosedale Ave *YO26* 16 D3
Rosedale St *YO10* 18 C5
Rosemary Ct *YO1* 5 G4
Rosemary Pl *YO1* 5 G4
Rosslyn St *YO30* 17 H1
Rougier St *YO1* 4 C3
Roundhill Link *YO30* 12 A3
Rowan Ave (N.Ears.) *YO32* 13 E2
Rowan Pl (N.Ears.) *YO32* 13 E1
Rowans, The (Skel.) *YO30* 11 F1
Rowley Ct (Ears.) *YO32* 8 C4
Rowntree Ave *YO30* 12 D5
Royal Chase (Drin.) *YO24* 24 D1
Royston Cl **2** (Stren.) *YO32* 9 H2
Ruby St **1** *YO23* 18 A6
Ruddings Cl (Haxby) *YO32* 7 H3
Runswick Ave *YO26* 16 C3
Rushwood Cl **2** (Haxby) *YO32* 8 B2
Russell Dr *YO30* 11 H5
Russell St *YO23* 18 A5
Russet Dr *YO31* 19 G2
Rutland Cl (Cop.) *YO23* 22 A1
Ryburn Cl **13** *YO30* 12 A3
Rycroft Cl *YO31* 14 B5
Rydal Ave *YO31* 19 F1
Ryde, The (Skel.) *YO30* 6 A6
Rye Cl (Wig.) *YO32* 7 H3
Ryecroft (Stren.) *YO32* 9 F5
Ryecroft Ave *YO24* 24 A2
Ryehill Cl **4** (N.Ears.) *YO32* 13 E1
Ryemoor Rd (Haxby) *YO32* 7 H3
Rylatt Pl *YO26* 16 C4

S

Sadberge Ct *YO10* 19 H4
Saddlebrook Ct *YO24* 24 A1
Saddlers Cl **1** (Cop.) *YO23* 22 B1
Saddlers Cl (Hunt.) *YO32* 13 G3
Sails Dr *YO10* 19 G4
St. Aelred's Cl **5** *YO31* 19 E3
St. Aidans Ct *YO10* 25 H1
St. Andrew Ct *YO1* 5 F3
St. Andrewgate *YO1* 5 E3
St. Andrew's Ct **13** *YO1* 5 F3
St. Ann's Ct *YO10* 18 C5
St. Aubyn's Pl *YO24* 17 H5
St. Barnabas Cl **10** *YO26* 17 G2
St. Benedict Rd *YO23* 4 D6
St. Catherines Cl (Skel.) *YO30* 6 B6
St. Catherines Pl *YO24* 4 A6
St. Clements Gro *YO23* 18 B5
St. Denys Rd *YO1* 5 F5
St. Edwards Cl *YO24* 24 D1
St. Georges Fld *YO10* 5 E6
St. Georges Pl *YO24* 17 G5
St. Giles Ct **6** *YO31* 4 D1
St. Giles Rd (Skel.) *YO30* 6 A6
St. Giles Way (Cop.) *YO23* 22 B2
St. Helen's Rd *YO24* 24 C1
St. Helens Sq **3** *YO1* 4 D3
St. James Cl *YO30* 11 H2
St. James Ct **4** *YO26* 17 H2
St. James Mt *YO23* 17 H5
St. James Pl *YO24* 17 E6
St. Johns Cres **7** *YO31* 18 C1
St. Johns St *YO31* 5 E1
St. Lawrence Ct (Hes.) *YO10* 26 D1
St. Leonards Pl *YO1* 4 D2
St. Lukes Gro *YO30* 12 C6
St. Margarets Ter **12** *YO1* 5 G4
St. Marks Gro *YO30* 11 H3
St. Martins La *YO1* 4 C4
St. Marys *YO30* 4 C1
St. Marys Cl **3** (Stren.) *YO32* 9 G3
St. Marys Cl (Wig.) *YO32* 7 H2
St. Marys Gro *YO10* 19 H3
St. Marys La *YO30* 4 C1
St. Mary's Ms **5** (Wig.) *YO32* 7 H2
St. Marys Sq **15** *YO1* 5 E4
St. Marys Ter *YO30* 4 C2
St. Maurices Rd *YO31* 5 F2
St. Nicholas Ave (Fulford) *YO19* 26 A5
St. Nicholas Cl (Cop.) *YO23* 22 A1
St. Nicholas Cres (Cop.) *YO23* 22 A1
St. Nicholas Cft (A.Bry.) *YO23* 22 D4
St. Nicholas Pl **4** *YO10* 19 E4
St. Nicholas Rd (Cop.) *YO23* 22 A1
St. Nicholas Way (Wig.) *YO32* 7 H2
St. Olaves Rd *YO30* 18 A1
St. Oswalds Rd *YO10* 25 H1
St. Pauls Ms *YO24* 17 H3
St. Pauls Sq *YO24* 17 G4
St. Paul's Ter *YO24* 17 H4
St. Peters Cl **5** (Knapton) *YO26* 16 B3
St. Peters Gro *YO30* 18 A1
St. Phillips Gro *YO30* 12 B5
St. Sampsons Sq *YO1* 5 E3
St. Saviourgate *YO1* 5 F3
St. Saviours Pl **2** *YO1* 5 F3
St. Stephen's Rd *YO24* 16 D6
St. Stephens Sq *YO24* 16 D6
St. Swithin's Wk *YO26* 17 F3
St. Thomas Pl **4** *YO31* 18 B1
St. Thomas's Cl *YO10* 19 H3
St. Wilfrids Cl **2** (Stren.) *YO32* 9 G6
St. Wilfrids Rd (Stren.) *YO32* 9 G6
St. Wulstans Cl *YO31* 13 F6
Salisbury Rd *YO26* 17 G2
Salisbury Ter *YO26* 17 G2
Salmond Rd *YO24* 16 C6
Sandacre Ct **1** *YO26* 17 E2
Sandcroft Cl *YO24* 24 B1
Sandcroft Rd *YO24* 24 B1
Sandholme (Haxby) *YO32* 8 B1
Sandmartin Ct *YO24* 24 B1
Sandown Ct *YO24* 17 E6
Sandringham Cl (Haxby) *YO32* 7 H4
Sandringham St *YO10* 18 C5
Sandstock Rd *YO31* 14 A6
Sandygap **7** (Haxby) *YO32* 7 H4
Sandyland (Haxby) *YO32* 7 H2
Sandyridge (N.Pop.) *YO26* 10 D4
Sargent Ave (Bish.) *YO23* 24 D5
Saville Gro *YO30* 12 B5
Sawyers Cres (Cop.) *YO23* 22 B1
Sawyers Wk (Dun.) *YO19* 21 H1
Saxford Way (Wig.) *YO32* 7 G1
Saxon Pl *YO31* 13 F6
Scafell Cl *YO30* 11 H4
Scaife Gdns **10** *YO31* 12 D6
Scaife Ms **9** *YO31* 12 D6
Scaife St *YO31* 12 D6
Scarborough Ter *YO30* 18 A1
Scarcroft Hill *YO24* 18 A5
Scarcroft La *YO23* 4 C6
Scarcroft Rd *YO23* 4 A6

Scarcroft Rd *YO24* 4 A6
Scaudercroft (Dun.) *YO19* 21 H1
Scawton Ave *YO31* 13 F3
School Cl (Skel.) *YO30* 6 B6
School La (Fulford) *YO10* 26 A2
School La (Hes.) *YO10* 19 G6
School La (A.Rich.) *YO23* 22 A4
School La (Bish.) *YO23* 25 E5
School La (Cop.) *YO23* 22 A2
School La (U.Pop.) *YO26* 10 C4
School St *YO24* 17 E4
Scott St *YO23* 18 B5
Scriven Gro (Haxby) *YO32* 8 B2
Scrope Ave *YO31* 18 D2
Seafire Cl *YO30* 12 B2
Seaton Cl **2** *YO10* 19 H3
Second Ave *YO31* 19 E1
Sefton Ave *YO31* 13 G5
Segrave Wk *YO26* 17 F3
Selby Rd (Fulford) *YO19* 26 A3
Seldon Rd *YO26* 17 F2
Seventh Ave *YO31* 19 E2
Severn Grn (N.Pop.) *YO26* 11 F5
Severus Ave *YO24* 17 E3
Severus St *YO24* 17 E4
Seymour Gro *YO31* 19 E1
Shallowdale Gro **5** *YO10* 19 H4
Shambles *YO1* 5 E3
Shaws Ter *YO24* 4 B6
Shelley Gro *YO30* 11 H5
Shelly Dr (Stren.) *YO32* 9 F4
Sherborne Gro **2** (Stren.) *YO32* 9 G4
Sheriff Hutton Rd (Stren.) *YO32* 9 G2
Sherringham Dr *YO24* 24 B1
Sherwood Gro (Acomb) *YO26* 16 C1
Sherwood Gro (Hunt.) *YO31* 13 G4
Shilton Garth Cl (Ears.) *YO32* 8 C4
Shipton Rd *YO30* 11 H4
Shipton St *YO30* 12 C6
Shirley Ave *YO26* 16 D1
Shotel Cl **5** *YO30* 12 A5
Silver St **8** *YO1* 5 E3
Silverdale Ct *YO24* 24 B2
Sim Balk La *YO23* 24 C4
Simons Cl (Stren.) *YO32* 9 F4
Sirocco Ct **7** *YO31* 13 E5
Sitwell Gro *YO26* 16 D2
Siward St *YO10* 19 F4
Sixth Ave *YO31* 19 E2
Skeldergate *YO1* 4 D4
Skeldergate Br *YO1* 5 E6
Skelton Ct **2** *YO30* 17 H1
Skelton La (Wig.) *YO32* 6 D2
Skewsby Gro *YO31* 13 G4
Skiddaw *YO24* 24 A2
Slessor Rd *YO24* 16 C6
Slingsby Gro *YO24* 24 C1
Smales St *YO1* 4 D5
Smary La (Murton) *YO19* 20 D1
Smeaton Gro *YO26* 16 D2
Smith Cl *YO10* 26 B1
Smithie Cl (N.Ears.) *YO32* 8 A6
Snowdon Cl (A.Rich.) *YO23* 22 A4
Somerset Cl *YO30* 11 H2
Somerset Rd **6** *YO31* 13 E6
South Bk Ave *YO23* 18 A6
South Esplanade *YO1* 5 E5
South La (Haxby) *YO32* 8 A2
South Par *YO23* 4 B5
South Vw Ter *YO24* 16 D4
Southdown Rd (Hunt.) *YO32* 8 C6
Southfield Cres *YO24* 24 C1
Southfields Rd (Stren.) *YO32* 9 G3
Southlands (Haxby) *YO32* 7 H1
Southlands Rd *YO23* 18 A5
Southolme Dr *YO30* 11 H5
Sowerby Rd *YO26* 17 E3
Spalding Ave *YO30* 12 B6
Speculation St *YO1* 5 G4
Spen La *YO1* 5 F3
Spencer St **3** *YO23* 4 D6
Spey Bk *YO24* 24 A3
Spindle Cl *YO24* 24 A1
Spinney, The *YO24* 24 D2
Spring Bk Ave (Dun.) *YO19* 21 G1
Spring La (Hes.) *YO10* 19 F6
Springfield Cl *YO31* 14 A6
Springfield Ct **7** *YO24* 17 G4
Springfield Rd (U.Pop.) *YO26* 10 C3
Springfield Way *YO31* 14 A6
Springwood (Haxby) *YO32* 8 A4
Spruce Cl **4** (N.Ears.) *YO32* 13 E3
Spurr Ct *YO24* 24 A1
Spurriergate **12** *YO1* 5 E4
Stabler Cl **1** (Wig.) *YO32* 7 F2
Stablers Wk (Ears.) *YO32* 8 C4
Staindale Cl *YO30* 11 H3
Staithes Cl **1** *YO26* 16 C3
Stakers Orchard (Cop.) *YO23* 22 B2
Stamford Br Rd (Dun.) *YO19* 20 D3
Stamford St E **5** *YO26* 17 G2
Stamford St W **2** *YO26* 17 G2
Stanley Ave (Haxby) *YO32* 8 A5
Stanley St *YO31* 18 C1
Starkey Cres *YO31* 19 E2
Station Ave *YO24* 4 C3
Station Ave (N.Ears.) *YO32* 13 E2
Station Ri *YO1* 4 B3
Station Ri *YO24* 4 B3
Station Rd (Cop.) *YO23* 22 A2
Station Rd *YO24* 4 C3
Station Rd (U.Pop.) *YO26* 10 C5
Station Rd (Haxby) *YO32* 8 B2
Station Sq (Stren.) *YO32* 9 G4
Steeple Cl **8** (Wig.) *YO32* 7 G1
Stephenson Cl (Hunt.) *YO32* 13 F4
Stephenson Way **14** *YO26* 17 G2
Sterne Ave *YO31* 19 F2
Stirling Gro *YO10* 26 B1
Stirling Rd *YO30* 12 A2
Stirrup Cl *YO24* 23 H1
Stockhill Cl (Dun.) *YO19* 21 G1
Stockholm Cl *YO10* 25 H1
Stockton La *YO31* 13 G6
Stockton La *YO32* 14 B4
Stone Riggs (St.For.) *YO32* 15 F1
Stonebow, The *YO1* 5 F3
Stonegate *YO1* 4 D3
Stonegate Wk *YO1* 4 D2
Stonelands Ct **5** *YO30* 12 B4
Stones Cl *YO24* 17 F5
Stonethwaite *YO24* 24 A2
Stoop Cl (Wig.) *YO32* 7 H3
Stow Ct (Hunt.) *YO32* 13 F2
Strakers Pas **7** *YO1* 5 F4
Stratford Way (Hunt.) *YO32* 13 F2
Stray Garth *YO31* 13 G6
Stray Rd *YO31* 19 G1
Straylands Gro *YO31* 13 G5
Strensall Pk (Stren.) *YO32* 9 E1
Strensall Rd (Ears.) *YO32* 8 D3
Strensall Rd (Hunt.) *YO32* 8 C6
Strensall Rd (Stren.) *YO32* 9 F6
Stuart Rd *YO24* 17 E5
Stubden Gro *YO30* 12 A3
Sturdee Gro *YO31* 13 E6
Summerfield Rd *YO24* 24 A2
Sunningdale Cl *YO26* 16 C2
Sunnydale (Haxby) *YO32* 8 A4
Surrey Way **2** *YO30* 12 A5
Surtees St *YO30* 12 C6
Sussex Cl *YO10* 19 H5
Sussex Rd *YO10* 19 H5
Sussex Way (Stren.) *YO32* 9 F4
Sutherland St *YO23* 18 A6
Sutor Cl (Cop.) *YO23* 22 B1
Sutton Rd (Wig.) *YO32* 7 F2
Sutton Way *YO30* 12 C5
Swale Ave *YO24* 24 C1
Swann St *YO23* 4 C6
Swarthdale (Haxby) *YO32* 8 B1
Swinegate *YO1* 5 E3
Swinegate Ct **1** *YO1* 5 E3
Swinerton Ave *YO26* 17 G1
Swinsty Ct **9** *YO30* 12 A4
Sycamore Ave (N.Ears.) *YO32* 13 F2
Sycamore Cl (Skel.) *YO30* 11 F1
Sycamore Cl (Haxby) *YO32* 8 A4
Sycamore Ct **11** (N.Ears.) *YO32* 13 F1
Sycamore Pl *YO30* 4 B1
Sycamore Pl **2** (N.Ears.) *YO32* 13 F1
Sycamore Ter *YO30* 4 B2
Sycamore Vw (U.Pop.) *YO26* 10 C4
Sykes Cl **3** *YO30* 18 A1

T

Tadcaster Rd *YO23* 24 D1
Tadcaster Rd (Drin.) *YO24* 24 C2
Tamworth Rd *YO30* 12 B4
Tang Hall La *YO10* 19 F3
Tang Hall La *YO31* 19 E2
Tanner Row *YO1* 4 C4
Tanners Moat **1** *YO1* 4 C3
Tarbert Cres *YO24* 23 H2
Tatton Cl *YO30* 12 B4
Teal Dr *YO24* 24 A1
Teck St **2** *YO23* 18 B5
Tedder Rd *YO24* 16 C6
Telford Ter *YO24* 18 A5
Temple Ave *YO10* 19 G3
Temple Garth (Cop.) *YO23* 22 C3
Temple La (Cop.) *YO23* 22 B3
Temple Rd (Bish.) *YO23* 24 D5
Templemead *YO31* 13 F5
Ten Thorn La *YO26* 16 B3
Tennent Rd *YO24* 16 C5
Tennyson Ave *YO30* 12 D6
Terrington Ct (Stren.) *YO32* 9 G2
Terry Ave *YO23* 5 E6
Terry St *YO23* 18 B6
Thackerays Yd *YO1* 5 G5
Thanet Rd *YO24* 17 E6
Thatchers Cft (Cop.) *YO23* 22 B1
Theresa Cl *YO32* 13 G4
Thief La *YO10* 19 F4
Third Ave *YO31* 19 E2
Thirkleby Way *YO10* 19 H3
Thirlmere Dr *YO31* 19 F1
Thomas St **1** *YO10* 18 D4
Thompson Pl **13** *YO26* 17 F2
Thoresby Rd *YO24* 16 C6
Thorn Nook *YO31* 13 F5
Thorncroft (Dun.) *YO19* 21 H1
Thornfield Ave *YO31* 13 G5
Thornfield Dr *YO31* 13 F4
Thornhills (Haxby) *YO32* 8 C2
Thornton Moor Cl **6** *YO30* 12 A3
Thorntree Gro *YO30* 12 B3
Thornwood Covert *YO24* 16 D6
Thorpe St *YO23* 18 A5
Tilmire Cl *YO10* 26 B1
Tisbury Rd *YO26* 17 F3
Tithe Cl *YO24* 16 C6
Toby Ct (Stren.) *YO32* 9 G4
Toft Grn *YO1* 4 B4
Top La (Cop.) *YO23* 22 A1
Toremil Cl **9** (N.Ears.) *YO32* 13 E1
Torridon Pl *YO24* 23 H2
Tostig Ave *YO26* 16 D2
Tower Pl *YO1* 5 E5
Tower St *YO1* 5 E5
Town End Gdns (Wig.) *YO32* 7 G1
Townend St *YO31* 18 B1
Towthorpe La (Tow.) *YO32* 9 E1
Towthorpe Rd (Haxby) *YO32* 8 C2
Towton Ave *YO24* 17 G5
Trafalgar St *YO23* 18 A6
Tranby Ave *YO10* 20 A3
Trenchard Rd *YO26* 16 C1
Trenfield Ct **6** *YO24* 17 G4
Trent Ave (Hunt.) *YO32* 8 C5
Trent Way *YO24* 24 B2
Trentholme Dr *YO24* 17 H5
Trevor Gro *YO24* 17 G5
Trinity La *YO1* 4 C4
Trinity Meadows (St.For.) *YO32* 15 G1
Troon Cl *YO26* 16 C2
Troutbeck *YO24* 24 A2
Troutsdale Ave *YO30* 11 H3
Tudor Rd *YO24* 16 D5
Tuke Ave *YO10* 19 G3
Turks Head Ct **3** *YO1* 5 E2

Turnberry Dr *YO26* 16 C3
Turners Cft (Hes.) *YO10* 26 C1
Turnmire Rd *YO24* 24 C1
Turpin Ct **5** *YO1* 5 F5
Twin Pike Way **2** (Wig.) *YO32* 7 G2
Tyneham Way **1** (Stren.) *YO32* 9 G4

U

Ullswater *YO24* 24 A2
Undercroft (Dun.) *YO19* 21 H1
Union Ter *YO31* 18 B1
University Rd (Hes.) *YO10* 19 E5
Upper Hanover St **1** *YO26* 17 G2
Upper Newborough St *YO30* 12 D6
Upper Price St *YO23* 18 A5
Upper St. Pauls Ter *YO24* 17 H3
Uppercroft (Haxby) *YO32* 7 H3
Usher La (Haxby) *YO32* 8 A2
Usher Pk Rd (Haxby) *YO32* 8 B1

V

Vale, The (Skel.) *YO30* 6 A6
Vanbrugh Dr *YO10* 19 H4
Vavasour Ct (Cop.) *YO23* 22 B2
Vernon Cl (Bish.) *YO23* 25 E6
Vernon Rd *YO30* 11 H3
Vesper Dr *YO24* 16 C4
Vesper Wk (Hunt.) *YO32* 8 C5
Vicarage Gdns **1** *YO10* 19 H3
Vicars Cl (Cop.) *YO23* 22 B2
Victor St *YO1* 4 D5
Victoria Bar *YO1* 4 C5
Victoria Ct *YO26* 17 G2
Victoria St **1** *YO23* 4 D6
Victoria Way (Hunt.) *YO32* 13 F4
Viking Rd *YO26* 16 D2
Villa Gro *YO31* 18 D1
Village, The (Skel.) *YO30* 6 A6
Village, The (Haxby) *YO32* 7 H2
Village, The (St.For.) *YO32* 15 F1
Village, The (Stren.) *YO32* 9 G3
Village, The (Wig.) *YO32* 7 G2
Village Garth (Wig.) *YO32* 7 H1
Vincent Way *YO24* 24 A1
Vine St *YO23* 18 B5
Vyner St *YO31* 12 D6

W

Waggoners Dr **3** (Cop.) *YO23* 22 B1
Waincroft (Stren.) *YO32* 9 F5
Wainers Cl **6** (Cop.) *YO23* 22 B1
Wains Gro *YO24* 24 B2
Wains Rd *YO24* 24 B1
Walker Dr *YO24* 23 H1
Walmer Carr (Wig.) *YO32* 7 F2
Walmgate *YO1* 5 G4
Walmgate *YO10* 5 G4
Walmgate Bar *YO1* 5 G5
Walney Rd *YO31* 19 F2
Walnut Cl *YO10* 19 F6
Walnut Cl **2** (Haxby) *YO32* 8 A2
Walpole St *YO31* 13 E6
Waltham Cl (Stren.) *YO32* 9 H2
Walton Pl *YO26* 16 C4
Walworth St **3** *YO26* 17 G2
Wandhill (Haxby) *YO32* 7 H3
Wandle, The *YO26* 16 B5
Wansbeck *YO24* 23 H3
Ward Ct *YO23* 4 D6
Warwick St *YO31* 13 E6
Wasdale Cl **10** *YO30* 11 H4
Water End *YO26* 17 F2
Water End *YO30* 17 G1
Water La (Dun.) *YO19* 21 H1
Water La *YO30* 12 B5
Waterdale Pk **4** *YO31* 13 F4
Waterings **3** (Wig.) *YO32* 7 G2
Waterman Ct *YO24* 16 C6
Watson St *YO24* 17 H4
Watson Ter *YO24* 17 H4
Wattlers Cl **7** (Cop.) *YO23* 22 B1
Waveney Gro **12** *YO30* 12 C5
Waverley St *YO31* 5 F1
Waynefleet Gro **3** *YO10* 19 F4
Weavers Cl (Cop.) *YO23* 22 B1
Weavers Pk (Cop.) *YO23* 22 B1
Weddall Cl *YO24* 17 G6
Welborn Cl *YO10* 19 F3
Welland Ri *YO26* 17 E2
Wellesley Cl *YO30* 12 B3
Wellington Row *YO1* 4 C3
Wellington St *YO10* 5 H6
Welton Ave *YO26* 17 E2
Welwyn Dr *YO10* 26 A1
Wenham Rd *YO24* 24 A1
Wenlock Ter *YO10* 18 C6
Wensleydale Dr *YO10* 20 A3
Wentworth Rd *YO24* 18 A5
Werkdyke, The **6** *YO1* 5 F2
West Bk *YO24* 17 F4
West End (Stren.) *YO32* 9 F4
West End Cl (Stren.) *YO32* 9 G3
West Moor La (Hes.) *YO10* 26 C1
West Nooks (Haxby) *YO32* 8 C2
West Thorpe *YO24* 24 B1
Westerdale Ct **1** *YO30* 17 H1
Western Ter **4** (Haxby) *YO32* 7 H1
Westfield Cl (U.Pop.) *YO26* 10 B5
Westfield Cl (Wig.) *YO32* 7 H2
Westfield Dr *YO10* 25 H1
Westfield Gro (Wig.) *YO32* 7 G2
Westfield La (U.Pop.) *YO26* 10 A4
Westfield La (Wig.) *YO32* 7 G2
Westfield Pl *YO24* 16 B6
Westfield Pl (Wig.) *YO32* 7 H2
Westfield Rd (Wig.) *YO32* 7 H2
Westholme Dr *YO30* 11 H4
Westlands Gro *YO31* 13 G6
Westminster Rd *YO30* 17 H1
Westpit La (Stren.) *YO32* 9 F4
Westview Cl *YO26* 11 E6
Westwood La (A.Bry.) *YO23* 22 D3
Westwood Ms **2** (Dun.) *YO19* 21 H1
Westwood Ter *YO23* 18 A6
Wetherby Rd *YO26* 16 B4
Wharfe Dr *YO24* 24 B1
Wharncliffe Dr **4** *YO30* 12 A3
Wharton Ave *YO30* 12 C6
Wheatcroft **1** (Stren.) *YO32* 9 F5
Wheatfield La (Haxby) *YO32* 7 H3
Wheatlands Gro *YO26* 16 D2
Wheatley Dr (Haxby) *YO32* 7 H3
Wheeldale Dr *YO32* 14 C3
Wheelwright Cl (Cop.) *YO23* 22 B2
Whenby Gro *YO31* 13 G4
Whernside Ave *YO31* 19 F2
Whin Cl *YO24* 24 D2
Whin Cl (Stren.) *YO32* 9 G5
Whin Garth *YO24* 24 D3
Whin Rd *YO24* 24 D3
Whip-Ma-Whop-Ma-Gate **8** *YO1* 5 F3
Whistler Cl (Cop.) *YO23* 22 C1
Whitby Ave *YO31* 13 H6
Whitby Dr *YO31* 13 H6
White Cross Rd *YO31* 13 E6
White Horse Cl **2** (Hunt.) *YO32* 8 C6
White Ho Dale *YO24* 17 G6
White Ho Dr *YO24* 17 G6
White Ho Gdns *YO24* 17 G6
White Ho Ri *YO24* 17 G6
White Rose Ave (N.Ears.) *YO32* 13 E2
White Rose Cl (N.Pop.) *YO26* 11 F4
White Rose Gro (N.Ears.) *YO32* 13 E2
White Rose Way (N.Pop.) *YO26* 11 E5
Whitelands (Ears.) *YO32* 8 C3
Whitestone Dr *YO31* 13 F3
Whitethorn Cl *YO31* 13 F3
Whitley Cl *YO30* 12 B4
Whitton Pl **4** *YO10* 19 H3
Wigginton Rd *YO31* 12 D4
Wigginton Rd *YO32* 12 C1
Wigginton Ter *YO31* 12 D6
Wilberforce Ave *YO30* 12 C6
Wilkinson Way (Stren.) *YO32* 9 F4
Willans Gro **4** *YO26* 17 F3
William Plows Ave *YO10* 18 D5
Willis St *YO10* 5 H6
Willoughby Way *YO24* 23 H1
Willow Bk (N.Ears.) *YO32* 13 F1
Willow Cft (U.Pop.) *YO26* 10 B5
Willow Glade (Hunt.) *YO32* 13 G2
Willow Gro *YO31* 13 G6
Willow Gro (Ears.) *YO32* 8 D4
Willowbank (N.Ears.) *YO32* 13 F2
Willows, The **1** *YO30* 12 C6
Willows, The (Stren.) *YO32* 9 G4
Wilsthorpe Gro *YO10* 26 B1
Wilstrop Fm Rd (Cop.) *YO23* 22 A2
Wilton Ms *YO24* 17 G4
Wilton Ri *YO24* 17 G4
Winchester Ave *YO26* 17 F3
Winchester Gro *YO26* 17 E3
Windermere *YO24* 24 B2
Windmill La *YO10* 19 G4
Windmill Ri *YO26* 17 F4
Windmill Way (Haxby) *YO32* 8 B2
Windsor Dr (Haxby) *YO32* 7 G1
Windsor Dr (Wig.) *YO32* 7 F1
Windsor Garth *YO24* 17 E6
Windsor St *YO23* 18 A6
Winscar Gro **2** *YO30* 11 H3
Winterscale Ct *YO10* 18 C5
Winterscale St *YO10* 18 C5
Witham Dr (Hunt.) *YO32* 8 D5
Woburn Cl (Stren.) *YO32* 9 H2
Wolfe Ave *YO31* 19 E2
Wolsey Dr (Bish.) *YO23* 25 E6
Wolsley St *YO10* 5 H6
Wolviston Ave *YO10* 19 G4
Wood Cl (Stren.) *YO32* 9 F4
Wood St *YO31* 18 D1
Wood Way (Hunt.) *YO32* 13 H1
Woodcock Cl **1** (Haxby) *YO32* 8 B2
Woodford Pl *YO24* 17 E6
Woodhouse Gro **1** *YO31* 19 F3
Woodland Chase *YO30* 12 C4
Woodland Pl (N.Ears.) *YO32* 13 F1
Woodland Way (Hunt.) *YO32* 13 G1
Woodlands Ave (Wig.) *YO32* 7 H3
Woodlands Gro *YO31* 13 H5
Woodlea Ave *YO26* 16 D3
Woodlea Bk *YO26* 16 D3
Woodlea Cres *YO26* 17 E3
Woodlea Gro *YO26* 16 D3
Woodleigh Cl (Stren.) *YO32* 9 F5
Woodside Ave *YO31* 19 F1
Woolnough Ave *YO10* 19 G4
Worcester Dr *YO31* 19 G2
Wordsworth Cres *YO24* 24 A2
Wrays Ave **6** *YO31* 13 F4
Wrays Cotts **5** *YO31* 13 F4
Wycliffe Ave *YO10* 19 G3
Wydale Rd *YO10* 20 A3

Y

Yarburgh Gro **12** *YO26* 17 F2
Yarburgh Way *YO10* 19 H4
Yearsley Cres *YO31* 13 E6
Yearsley Gro *YO31* 13 F4
Yew Tree Ms (Osb.) *YO10* 19 H2
York Bypass *YO10* 26 D4
York Bypass *YO19* 14 D4
York Bypass *YO23* 24 D4
York Castle *YO1* 5 F5
York Rd (Dun.) *YO19* 21 E3
York Rd (Acomb) *YO24* 16 D4
York Rd *YO26* 16 D4
York Rd (Haxby) *YO32* 8 A4
York Rd (Stren.) *YO32* 9 G3
York St (Dun.) *YO19* 21 F2